You
Are the
President

YOU
ARE THE
PRESIDENT

Nathan Aaseng

The Oliver Press, Inc.
Minneapolis

The Oliver Press
Charlotte Square
5707 West 36th Street
Minneapolis, MN 55416-2510

Library of Congress Cataloging-in-Publication Data

Aaseng, Nathan.
You are the president / Nathan Aaseng.
p. cm.— (Great decisions)
Includes bibliographical references and index.
ISBN 1-881508-10-2
1. United States—Politics and government—20th century—
Decision making—Juvenile literature.
2. United States—Foreign relations—20th century—Decision
making—Juvenile literature.
3. Presidents—United States—Decision making—Juvenile
literature.
[1. Presidents. 2. United States—Politics and government—20th
century. 3. Decision making.]
I. Title. II. Series.

E743.A16   1994   93-5776
973.9—dc20   CIP
                                         AC

ISBN: 1-881508-10-2
Great Decisions I
Printed in the United States of America

04 03 02 01 00 99 98   8 7 6 5 4 3 2

CONTENTS

Introduction...7

Chapter 1   Pennsylvania Coal Strike:
              October 1902...9

Chapter 2   Covenant of the League of Nations:
              August 1919...25

Chapter 3   Entangling Alliances:
              December 1940 45

Chapter 4   To End the War:
              Summer 1945 61

Chapter 5   Race Riot in Little Rock:
              September 1957......................................77

Chapter 6   The Nuclear Edge:
              October 1962..93

Chapter 7   Southeast Asia:
              June 1965 111

Chapter 8   A Third-Rate Burglary:
              June 1972 131

Source Notes 153

Bibliography 154

Index 155

Harry Truman made many of the most difficult decisions of the twentieth century. "The Buck Stops Here" sign on his White House desk reminded him that, as the president, he alone was responsible for those decisions.

INTRODUCTION

The weight of the world crushes down on your shoulders. A crisis demands a decision that will affect the lives of millions of people and perhaps alter the course of history.

You are the one who must make that decision, for you are the president of the United States.

No one can make the decision for you. You can study reports and charts and listen to expert advice until your eyes glaze over, but these experts are not you—the president. The decision is not theirs to make. As President Harry Truman was fond of saying, "The buck stops here."

The choices are not easy. Traps and pitfalls await you in these complex issues. You dare not make a mistake, and yet you must do something. Everyone is counting on you.

Welcome to the world of the president! This book allows you to sit behind the desk at the Oval Office of the White House and experience the challenge of solving some of the country's toughest problems. You will encounter eight actual crises faced by eight different U.S. presidents in the twentieth century. Advisers will summarize the situation for you and then present you with options. Your job is to handle each crisis by choosing one of these options.

After you have done so, you will see what the real president did in these situations and why he made the choice he did. Then you will discover what happened as a result of that decision. Finally, to help you evaluate the wisdom of the president's choice, each chapter presents a hindsight section evaluating the president's decision. In other words, given the benefit of knowing how events unfolded, was the president's choice a wise one? Presidents make mistakes just like everyone else, and you will find that some of these decisions did not work out the way the presidents had planned. Perhaps you will find evidence that the choice you made would have worked better than the choice made at the time.

The eight crises span the first three-quarters of the twentieth century. They include domestic and foreign crises faced by both Democratic and Republican presidents. These crises were selected for their impact on the goals and effectiveness of the presidents' administrations.

It is easy to sit back and criticize a presidential decision. Now prepare to jump back into history and discover what it is like to be the president who has to make the decisions.

1

PENNSYLVANIA COAL STRIKE

October 1902

The greatest work stoppage in the history of the United States threatens to plunge the nation into chaos and class warfare. Nearly 150,000 coal miners in Pennsylvania walked off their jobs on May 12. Their action has virtually shut down the entire anthracite coal industry. Anthracite (a hard form of coal) is the primary energy source for much of the country, particularly the industrial Northeast.

The strike has dragged on into its fifth month. Each day, the coal bins grow emptier while the frigid temperatures of winter crowd ever closer. Prices have skyrocketed as people scramble to buy up what little reserves of coal are left. The strike has priced the poor and even the middle class out of the fuel market. A ton of coal that sold for less than $3.00 a year ago now fetches more than $30.00.

Already, schools in Massachusetts have begun to close. Others in New York and the rest of New England will soon follow suit. Even in the West, where the fuel situation is not as serious as in the East, mobs have hijacked railroad cars carrying coal through towns. Soon desperation will trigger panic, and riots will erupt throughout the country.

Unfortunately, there is no hope that the striking coal miners and the coal mine owners can reach a settlement in the near future. The owners refuse to deal with the miners, and the miners refuse to work under the present conditions. Both sides in the dispute have turned down proposed plans and compromises. They have also refused to listen to all appeals to their patriotism or their concern for the welfare of the country. Both sides are begging you—the president of the United States—to get involved and to take action on their behalf.

The mayor of New York City and the governor of Massachusetts have warned that their communities stand on the edge of catastrophe. Henry Cabot Lodge, the influential United States senator from Massachusetts, has warned you, "If no settlement is reached, it means political disaster. The public will take it out on you." On the other hand, the people are so desperate for coal that they will likely back any strong actions you take to end the strike, even actions that violate the Constitution of the United States. Each day that the strike continues, winter, riots, and chaos loom ever closer.

BACKGROUND

In the past few years, a few large coal-carrying railroad companies have bought most of the anthracite mines. Six railroad corporations, which now own more than 70 percent of the mines, are driving the smaller companies out of business by charging them high rates for hauling coal.

This small group of powerful railroad industrialists believes strongly in the rights of individuals to run their businesses as they see fit. Just two years earlier, the coal miners had threatened to strike. At that time, government and business leaders pressured the mine owners to give the miners a raise in pay. After granting that raise against their will, the owners are now furious that the miners are asking for more. The railroad executives resent both the earlier outside interference and the fact that the miners have banded together into a union to increase their bargaining power. This time, the owners are determined to hold onto their rights. Pointing out that the coal industry is not as profitable as it was even a few years before, they insist that they cannot afford to stay in business if they increase wages again.

The miners reply that mining is such a brutal occupation, no one can continue to work at it without some hope for improvement. Hours are long and hard, and the work is dangerous. Accidents kill 6 out of every 1,000 miners on the job each year; many more suffer serious injury. Those who survive rarely reach the age of 50 without severe health problems, such as asthma or lung and heart diseases. Frequent accidents leave many families depending on 11- and 12-year-old children to work grueling 12-hour shifts to keep the family alive.

Furthermore, the pay is low, and cost of living increases ate up their last pay raise. Out of their meager wages, miners must also pay for their own materials, such as blasting powder. In addition, if the quality of the coal they mine is poor, the company can dock their pay for "unmarketable coal." According to a priest in a mining community, miners are "barely able to exist. Homes are not really what we call homes, they are simply habitations."

Before the age of oil and gasoline, coal miners worked long hours under harsh conditions to provide the country with essential winter fuel.

The majority of the miners want a 20 percent wage increase and their work day reduced to eight hours. John Mitchell, president of the United Mine Workers union, lowers the wage demand to 5 percent. The mine operators reject any change in the work arrangement and refuse to recognize the union as a lawful negotiating group.

Mitchell and the miners then ask for outside arbitration to settle their differences with the owners. Still smarting over the last outside interference, the owners flatly refuse either to negotiate with the union or to accept arbitration. In the words of George Baer, the most outspoken of the mine owners, the owners would "not waste time negotiating with anarchists and criminals."

As president, you try reasoning with both parties. You invite representatives from the mine owners and the miners to the White House for a meeting. Your meeting accomplishes nothing.

William Stone, the governor of Pennsylvania, tries taking aggressive action. Hoping that many miners would return to work if the state would guarantee them protection from possible union violence, Stone orders the state militia to safeguard mine workers. That, too, accomplishes nothing. Virtually all miners stay on strike.

THE DECISION IS YOURS.

What action will you take to end this crisis?

Option 1 Send federal troops to break the strike.

The mine owners are asking you to intervene to break the strike. They request that you send an army to the mines to secure control, arrest the leaders of the United Mine Workers, prosecute them in the federal courts, and force the miners to return to work.

These are drastic actions, but then the severity of the crisis demands drastic actions. If coal does not start flowing in the country soon, there may be no country. Even many of those who are sympathetic with the miners believe that looking after the public good is more important than satisfying the miners' demands.

You are told there are many valid reasons to enter the dispute on the side of the mine owners. First, the United States was founded on the ideals of individual liberty. Most of the population considers the right of employers to operate their own businesses as almost sacred. Arguing against the unions, the mine owners believe it is the "right of every man to sell his labor in the free market." This means that employers are free to offer whatever conditions of employment they choose and that workers are free either to accept or to reject these offers.

In this case, the mine owners claim they should be free to mine coal or to stop mining coal as they please, to pay wages they decide on, and to exact any hours or conditions of work that they decree. Miners can take the offer or move on.

Most Americans believe that unions infringe on this freedom. They do not believe anyone has the right to come into a business, hold the employer hostage, and demand a say in matters of management. "There cannot be two masters in the management of business," states George Baer. Most Americans think employers should not have to deal with a union if they do not want to do so.

Another ideal that Americans hold dear is a belief in improving themselves through hard work. By trying to restrict the number of working hours in a day, the union is denying hardworking individuals the freedom to better themselves by working as many hours as they wish to work.

In taking action on behalf of the employers, you will be following the example set by earlier presidents. Historically, the federal government has always protected the property rights of owners. Most recently, in 1894,

Financier George Baer (1842-1914) believed that the mine owners, not their employees—the coal miners— should decide how to run the mines.

President Grover Cleveland ordered federal troops to forcibly break up a strike against the Pullman railroad operators.

The American public has traditionally supported this type of action. Basically, the federal government has a duty to preserve order. This strike has thrown the country into disorder. Many observers report continual violence and mob behavior on the part of the miners. One recent newspaper editorial declares, "It is not a coal strike but an insurrection."

If you do not immediately squelch this kind of undisciplined mob rule, the security of the nation will be threatened. The first order of business is to restore law and order to the mining communities so that owners and miners can work out their problems.

Option 2 **Send federal troops to seize and operate the mines.**

From your consideration of **Option 1,** it is clear that you need to intervene immediately. The country needs the coal desperately. But rather than step in on the side of the mine owners, you should take action *against* them.

Businesses dealing in products that affect the security of the entire country cannot claim the right to do whatever they please regardless of the consequences. Increasingly obvious to most observers is the fact that the owners are the ones who are blocking a settlement.

The owners' extremely harsh, arrogant stand has even outraged many of their former allies. Typical of their attitude is George Baer's declaration that God is on the side of the mine owners. These owners, he says, are the "Christian men to whom God in His infinite wisdom has given control of the property interests of the country." Furthermore, the owners have shown contempt for foreign-born workers who make up nearly half of the mining work force. Responding to complaints about the brutal working conditions, one owner said the miners "don't suffer, why they can't even speak English."

This attitude has caused former President Cleveland, who had ordered in troops to help railroad owners put down the Pullman strike, to distance himself from the mine operators. Cleveland has written a letter to you in which he says he is "especially disturbed by the tone and substance of the operators." As president, you have experienced that tone and substance yourself. At the White House meeting you arranged to discuss the situation, observers were shocked by the rude, insulting behavior of the mine owners.

The public, meanwhile, generally agrees that the mine workers, who have repeatedly agreed to abide by the decision of an impartial commission, have presented their case calmly and civilly. Contrary to the claims of the owners and several newspaper editorials, the mine workers have avoided violence during their strike. The Reverend James Moore, who lives in the middle of the coal mining country, declares, "I never saw a more peaceable community in my life." The fact that almost no miners showed up for work, even after the Pennsylvania militia came in to offer protection to returning workers, offers strong evidence that miners are backing the union of their own free will, not because of intimidation by the union.

The behavior of the miners, together with John Mitchell's reasoned appeals for fair play, have won unprecedented public support for this union. Never before in American history has a labor union disrupted such an important industry without raising a firestorm of public hostility.

Even those who do not care for unions cannot help but sympathize with the miners. Senator Lodge has written you asking if there is any form of pressure that can be put on the operators "who are driving us to ruin." The mayors of more than 100 cities have gone on record in support of government control of the mines. Respected New York lawyer Edward Lauterbach has studied the case and has concluded that the government has a legal right to intervene to "stop the wanton waste and fast-approaching inhumanity to the masses."

An Illinois miner from the age of 12, John Mitchell (1870-1919) became president of the United Mine Workers of America (1898-1908) and vice president of the American Federation of Labor (1899-1914).

Option 3 **Stay out of the dispute.**

Painful as the crisis is, federal government action will only make it worse. Sending troops to break the strike puts you on the side of the big coal owners who have acted so arrogantly. Sending troops to take over the mines, whatever lawyers like Lauterbach say, is dangerous and may be illegal.

The Constitution contains nothing that allows the federal government to seize private property without due process of law. If you declare that the government has the right to do so in this case, what is to prevent government officials from taking private property whenever they feel like it for whatever reason?

Your administration has already upset influential members of the business community by filing lawsuits against large corporations. Recently your justice department won a case in which they charged the Northern Securities Corporation with gaining unfair competitive advantage against rivals. Another radical action against business owners could throw the business community into an uproar and cause havoc with the economy.

The owners of the coal mines are confident that the miners will give in soon and that the crisis will be ended without you having to get involved.

Option 4 **Pressure both sides to negotiate a settlement.**

The crisis is too serious to do nothing. The public is pleading for you to do something. But rather than take drastic action, you could take the more moderate route of putting pressure on both sides to work out an agreement.

The miners are open to a negotiated settlement and are willing to let you appoint a commission to decide the issues. You have heard reports that, in exchange for some improvement in working conditions, the miners will give up their demands that the owners recognize their union.

The mine owners are the ones you will have to work on. They are determined to resist outside interference. To get them to budge, you will have to use some kind of threat, such as a promise to send troops to seize the mines if an agreement is not reached soon.

If you do make a threat like that, you had better be ready to back it up. According to observers, the owners "speak as though no power on earth can or will move them." If the owners keep digging in their heels, you may be backing yourself into a corner that will force you to seize the mines whether you want to or not.

YOU ARE THE PRESIDENT.
WHAT IS YOUR DECISION?

Option 1	**Send federal troops to break the strike.**
Option 2	**Send federal troops to seize and operate the mines.**
Option 3	**Stay out of the dispute.**
Option 4	**Pressure both side to negotiate a settlement.**

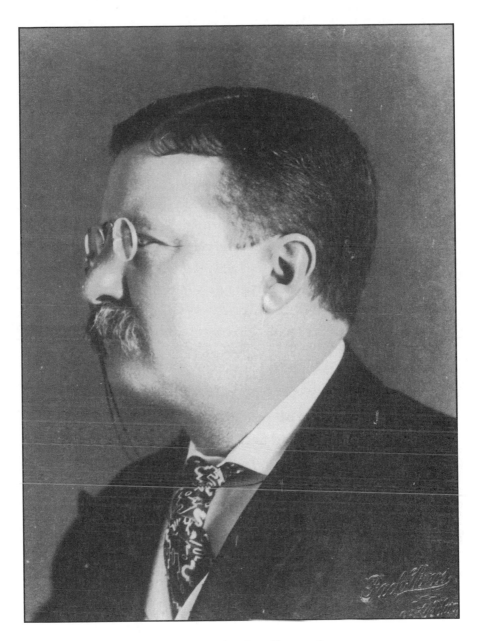

Republican President Theodore Roosevelt (1858-1919) had to deal with one of the bitterest labor crises in U.S. history.

President Theodore Roosevelt chose *Option 4*.

Roosevelt believed that the president, as "steward of the people," should take dynamic action in times of great crisis. As a result, he was extremely frustrated by the fact that "in theory" he had "no power to act directly." At one point he conceded, "I am at my wit's end how to proceed."

Roosevelt decided to make every effort to avoid federal intervention. But when all other possibilities failed, he said, "I could no more see misery and death come to the great masses . . . and sit by idly . . . than I could sit idly and see one man kill another without interference." He was prepared to do whatever necessary to get the mines back in operation and to spare the country riots and famine.

Roosevelt had a "horror of anarchy and disorder and pandering to the mob" that might have nudged him toward the side of the owners. But this was overridden in the end by his sense of compassion and fair play. Roosevelt once said, "It is better for the government to help a poor man make a living for his family than to help a rich man make more profit for his company."

Roosevelt let both sides know that unless they reached a settlement soon, he would send in federal troops to run the mines and would dictate his own settlement. He ordered Major General J. M. Schofield to prepare to take charge of the operation. Even Secretary of State Elihu Root wondered if Roosevelt were just bluffing. Yet Root admitted that the president had the nerve to back up his threat if necessary.

RESULT

Roosevelt's threat jolted the mine owners into softening their hard line. They agreed to let an independent commission arbitrate the dispute. The mine owners insisted, however, that the commission include certain types of professionals, including a federal judge and a mining engineer. The owners expected most of these commissioners to favor their cause.

Since the owners refused to recognize the union, they objected to any union representative being on the commission.

Roosevelt agreed to most of their terms and went as far as to accept three of the five specific individuals proposed by the owners. The miners, however, insisted on having a union miner on the commission. Roosevelt agreed this was fair but found that the owners were "prepared to sacrifice all and see civil war in the country" rather than give the union a place on the commission.

After hours of futile pleading, Roosevelt broke the gridlock with an ingenious compromise. When the owners agreed to have a "sociologist" as one of the professionals on the commission, Roosevelt simply appointed a union miner as the "sociologist."

With the announcement of the commission, the miners immediately returned to the mines. Coal supplies were renewed, and the country avoided a winter crisis.

Five months later, the commission recommended a ten percent wage increase for miners, a reduction of the work day to nine hours, and an end to some abusive management practices.

HINDSIGHT

Legal scholars have criticized as unconstitutional Theodore Roosevelt's stated intention of taking over the mines. Franklin D. Roosevelt, a college student at the time, thought government intervention in the case was a "serious mistake" that would give too much power to the federal government.

Historians, however, concede that Theodore Roosevelt's handling of the coal strike was a masterful use of presidential power. Roosevelt showed courage in breaking with the traditional use of federal troops as strikebreakers, restraint in holding back the troops, firmness in bringing the owners to the bargaining table, and creativity in solving the dispute over who was to be on the commission.

Roosevelt's actions demonstrated how government could be used as a balance to counter the growing power of narrow interest groups. His actions in fending off what he later described as the "certainty of riots and famine which might have developed into social war" earned him enormous prestige and public trust. Roosevelt used this popularity as a launching pad for a bold program of government action and regulation that he called the "Square Deal."

2

COVENANT OF THE LEAGUE OF NATIONS
August 1919

The great war in Europe is now over. The arrival of American troops midway through the war turned the tide and caused the defeat of Germany and its allies. But the staggering cost of the effort has dimmed the glow of victory. Nearly 9 million soldiers lost their lives in this war.

Determined that the horrible carnage of this war should never be repeated, you conceive a peacekeeping organization called the League of Nations. The League would combine the forces of all the nations in a solemn pact to guarantee international rights and laws. You hope that the moral force provided by this effort will make future wars impossible.

You have worked hard on this, and your leadership in securing victory, in promoting a just peace, and in building a League of Nations has made you the hero of the world. While you were on tour in Paris, Rome, and London shortly after the war, enormous crowds greeted you with cheers such as have never before been heard by any living person. You have been proclaimed the "Champion of the Rights of Man." Veteran observers report that they have never seen a time when so much hope filled the air.

You returned home in early summer to present the Covenant of the League of Nations to the United States Senate for approval. In this country, the League has strong support, both from state government officials and from newspaper editors. But despite this support and despite your international status as a hero, you find trouble brewing in the Senate. A group of powerful senators led by majority leader Henry Cabot Lodge of Massachusetts is determined to reject the Covenant of the League of Nations or at least to limit the involvement of the United States in it. If these senators succeed, they will deal a humiliating blow to your international peace efforts.

BACKGROUND

Although a majority of Americans support the general idea of the League of Nations, a strong vein of suspicion runs through the country. Americans reluctantly became involved in Europe's war. Now the European countries show no sign of having learned from their terrible war;

A typical scene of bleakness from the French battlefields of World War I

they are squabbling as much as ever. Many Americans are fed up with Europe's endless bickering and would be content to let these countries stew in their own mess. Americans are especially sensitive to the argument that the League of Nations would, as one League opponent says, "hand over American destiny to the secret councils of Europe."

To siphon support away from the Covenant, staunch opponents of the League, such as Senator William Borah of Idaho, have tapped into this suspicion. Borah asked, "Is there an American who wants a foreign nation to say when and where the Monroe Doctrine should apply?"

Some Americans believe that the League is just a big business scheme meant to involve their country in another profitable war.

Furthermore, critics are suspicious of your motives. You have spent a great deal of time in Europe, settling Europe's problems and trying to set up the League of Nations. During this time, you have ignored domestic problems in the United States. Your opponents accuse you of being power hungry and engaging in a "campaign for the Presidency of the Federation of the World."

When the Senate votes on the Covenant of the League of Nations, the numbers will work against you. According to the Constitution, all treaties must be approved by two-thirds of the Senate in order to become law. The opposing political party holds a majority of the seats in the Senate. Thus, even if every senator in your party votes with you, you will still need to persuade many members of the opposition to support the Covenant.

Gaining the opposition's support may be possible, however, as many of the opposition describe themselves as "mild reservationists" on this issue. That is, they have some misgivings about the League of Nations, but given some assurances from you that the United States' right to decide its own course will be safeguarded, they are likely to vote in favor of the Covenant.

The primary stumbling block is Article X of the Covenant. This article states that all League members must pledge to defend the political independence of member states and protect them in the case of outside attack. You view this article as the key to your peace plan. It is designed to discourage any country from attacking

A clever and influential politician, conservative Republican Henry Cabot Lodge (1850-1924) served Massachusetts in the U.S. Senate for 30 years.

another. Opponents, however, worry that this article will cause the United States to get dragged into countless spats between warring factions around the world.

Given the general support for the League of Nations around the country, one wouldn't think that convincing the mild reservationists would be difficult. Unfortunately, you cannot expect much cooperation from your opponents, and you can certainly expect none from Senator Lodge. The differences between the two of you are personal as well as political. You and Lodge have been bitter enemies ever since you took office. Quite apart from his feelings about the League, he would like nothing better than to defeat and even humiliate you. Lodge has lined up a parade of witnesses to testify against the League Covenant before the Senate Foreign Relations Committee that he chairs.

Lodge is a shrewd rival who knows better than to try to tackle the power and popularity of the president head on. He plans to attach so many amendments to the original version that it will no longer be effective. Additionally, Lodge knows that you would then have to go back to all the other signatories and renegotiate his amendments with them. Considering how hard you had to work to get the squabbling Europeans to agree the first time, this might kill the League.

As for the mild reservationists, you have made mistakes that could contribute to their reluctance to cooperate. You did not involve any high-ranking member of the opposition party in formulating the charter for the League of Nations. You, yourself, did all of the negotiating on the charter with the European nations. This has angered many senators who now feel that you view them as nothing more than rubber stamps to approve your programs. Also, in a speech you made on February 28, you attacked your opponents, calling them "blind and little provincial people" and saying they "have not got even good working imitations of minds."

Recently, in an attempt to appear more accommodating, you have been meeting with senators on an individual basis to discuss the League Covenant and to persuade them of its worth without changes. But as August drags on, you do not appear to be making much headway in gathering the votes you need.

Given the obstacles, this negotiation requires all the energy and skill you can muster. Right now, however, your energy is severely limited by health problems. You have had a long history of ailments, such as neuritis and respiratory problems, that have threatened your career from time to time. Your latest severe bout of illness began in Paris back in April when you were trying to negotiate honorable terms of peace to end the war in Europe. These negotiations forced you to work long hours dealing with the endless hassles and schemings of the European negotiators who were trying to grab the best deal they could.

The effort of trying to steer a path of international justice and peace through waters roiled by demands of selfish parties exhausted you. Doctors begged you to slow down, but you kept on—weary, haggard, gaunt.

Finally, on April 3, 1919, you fell seriously ill with a burning fever. Doctors diagnosed this as a case of the flu that has killed millions of people over the years. Although you have bounced back from that illness, you never had time to recover fully. Your weakness and lack of stamina occasionally show in your public appearances.

The Covenant of the League of Nations is due to come up for a vote in the Senate soon, and your chances of getting it passed without any changes appear dim.

THE DECISION IS YOURS.

Faced with these imposing odds against passage of the Covenant of the League of Nations without changes, what will you do?

Option 1 **Take your case to the people to win approval.**

Your reputation as a wartime victor and as a champion of peace has earned you great popularity among the masses. Rather than butt heads with a hostile Senate, take advantage of your popularity and rally the people to your cause. Let the people prove the power of democracy and put pressure on the senators. This could be done with a nationwide railway tour filled with speeches and rallies in support of the League.

This appeal to the people is something you have done successfully throughout your entire political career. In fact, some people have called your term as governor of New Jersey "one long series of appeals from the stump."

This strategy plays to your strengths. Political observers consider you to be one of the outstanding public speakers of your time. Your background as a college debate coach and 20 years of experience as a teacher at Princeton University is evident in every speech you give. Given a topic about which you are passionately concerned, you should be at the top of your form. A recent Memorial Day speech that you delivered on the League of Nations bears this out. One journalist called it the greatest speech he had ever heard in his life. Your speaking ability, added to your enormous popularity, almost guarantees that you can win the support of your listeners.

This approach, however, has several possible problems. This aggressive strategy may backfire. The Senate has a reputation for being less sensitive than other governing bodies to public opinion. They may actually resent the fact that you tried to "go over their heads" to the people and may stand even more firmly against you. In fashioning arguments strong enough to light a fire under the people, you may also risk saying things that

President Woodrow Wilson (standing in car)
campaigns through the streets of America.

would offend the mild reservationists and push them away
from compromising with you.

Also, the country faces many challenges—unem-
ployment, labor relations, and a soaring cost of living.
While spending all that time in Europe earlier this year,
you left these and many other important issues on the
back burner. Another month spent on a speaking tour

would only add to the backlog of important government work.

Finally, there is your health. In order for your trip to have any impact, you will need to go at a hard pace— visiting many cities, making many speeches. You would be spending nearly a month on the road without a break, bounced and rattled on railroad cars, battling the September heat. The task would be daunting enough for a person in good health. For a sickly person who has not fully recovered from a serious illness, this could be dangerous. Both your doctor and your wife advise you not to go.

Option 2 **Work out the best compromise you can with the Senate.**

Republican Senator James Watson has put the situation to you in stark terms: "Mr. President, you are licked. There is only one way you can take the United States into the League of Nations. Accept it with the Lodge reservations."

If you lose on this issue, the United States will not join the League. You would end up with the ultimate embarrassment of being the world leader who started an organization that his own government would not join. Worse, the League of Nations probably could not function effectively without the support of the most powerful nation on earth. You are convinced that only this organization can prevent terrible wars such as the world just endured and can guarantee justice and security in the world.

Some of your most trusted advisers, such as Edward Mandell House, have advised you that half a loaf is better

*President Wilson (right) with Texan Edward M.
House (1858-1938), his closest adviser*

than none at all, even if compromising means giving in to Lodge—your hated enemy. After studying the Lodge reservations to the Covenant, House said that the League's "practical workings in the future would not be seriously hampered" by these reservations. Another adviser argues that "people in the future will forget the minor disagreements if the [League] itself comes into being." Even the British ambassador to the United States believes that the "important thing is for America to come in."

On the other hand, what would happen if the United States attached conditions to its entrance into the League? What would prevent every country from deciding to do the same? The result would be chaos and a League so splintered that it could not function.

Furthermore, you have already tried to accommodate the reservations of suspicious Americans. During negotiations in Europe, people such as former President William H. Taft urged you to amend the League Covenant to protect U.S. interests. They assured you that this would erase any doubts Americans had. Against your wishes, you agreed to include such features as the right to withdraw from the League at any time and a guarantee that the League would not involve itself in domestic issues within a country. Now critics are back with further reservations and objections. This does not speak well for American faithfulness.

Most importantly, you signed your name to the Covenant of the League of Nations. That means you accepted it as is. You are long past the stage of rewriting the treaty. If you agree to changes and conditions now, that would be as good as going back on your word.

Option 3 **Withdraw the treaty proposal for the time being.**

Rather than risk everything on a vote now, you might delay action on the matter. Because of your poor health, you have not been able to use your powers of persuasion and negotiation to the fullest. Given time to recover fully, you might be able to do better. A little more time might also give you a chance to improve your tense relations with the Senate.

On the other hand, the League of Nations needs the United States urgently. Even now, violence is breaking out in many corners of the world. Turks and Russians are attacking Armenians. Poles and Ukrainians are heading for a showdown. Hostilities are brewing between Rumania and Hungary.

The League needs to be solidified quickly while the horror of the war is still fresh in everyone's mind. Delay could end any chance of getting it established. Already domestic issues are pushing the League of Nations off of center stage in the United States. Although Americans still support the League, they are no longer as passionate about it as they were at the end of the war.

Option 4 **Plead your case as best you can to the Senate and leave the vote to them.**

In working for peace, you have already taken on more than anyone could expect. You cannot do everything yourself. The Senate must now consider the Covenant. Rather than waste time on a barnstorming tour of the country, simply persuade the senators as well as you can. Rather than compromise and go back on your word to the Europeans, stick to your principles. If the Senate refuses to listen to reason, at least you can maintain your dignity in defeat.

Even an honorable defeat is hard to accept, however, when you have heard the voices of the people responding to your call for peace. You are the man who speaks for hundreds of millions of people who are sick of war. These people are counting on you to make the world safer so that their sons and daughters do not have to die the way so many did in the past few years. You also carry the burden of the deaths of thousands of American troops you sent to war in Europe. You sent them because you wanted this to be a "war to end all wars." But if the League does not grow strong enough to become an effective force, wars will continue to break out. Then will those soldiers you sent to war have died in vain?

YOU ARE THE PRESIDENT. WHAT IS YOUR DECISION?

Option 1   **Take your case to the people to win approval.**

Option 2   **Work out the best compromise you can with the Senate.**

Option 3   **Withdraw the treaty proposal for the time being.**

Option 4   **Plead your case as best you can to the Senate and leave the vote to them.**

Woodrow Wilson (1856-1924), 28th president of the United States, served as president of Princeton University and governor of New Jersey before entering the White House in 1913.

President Woodrow Wilson chose *Option 1*.

The League of Nations was desperately important to Wilson. He was certain that another major war would erupt within the next decade or two unless the countries of the world took strong measures to stop this from happening. He saw the League as the only way to enforce justice and peace in the world. "The League of Nations is now in its crisis, and if it fails I hate to think of what will happen to the world," he said. With so much at stake, Wilson was determined to do everything in his power to bring the United States into the League.

At the same time, Wilson would not compromise his position. "I have no moral right to compromise on a paper I already signed," he insisted. That option was all the more repulsive because it meant giving in to his hated rival, Lodge. In rejecting Lodge's reservations, Wilson said, "I'll never consent to adopt any policy with which that impossible name is so prominently identified. I'll appeal to the country."

Delay, too, was out of the question. This was "not a time for tactics," Wilson said. "It is time to stand square." As for concerns about his health, he insisted, "I don't care if I die the next minute after the treaty is ratified."

On the evening of September 2, 1919, President Wilson started out on a 27-day, coast-to-coast train trip to rally the American people in support of his League of Nations. His grueling schedule called for 30 major speeches in 26 cities plus many more shorter speeches from the rear platform of the train.

RESULT

Although the tour started out slowly, by the time it reached the West Coast, the strategy seemed to be working. Ever larger, more enthusiastic crowds turned out to cheer Wilson as he presented his case. The tour was building support for the League exactly as planned.

But the stress of the trip and the constant demands on his time took its toll on the president. Each day Wilson grew more exhausted, his nerves fraying toward the breaking point.

Late on the night of September 25, following a speech in Pueblo, Colorado, Wilson suffered what was described as a complete nervous breakdown. His doctor convinced him to cancel the rest of the tour. A week later, the president suffered a stroke. Paralyzed on one side, he hovered near death. For the next five months, he lay in bed, unable to deal with the business of the country.

At a time when his political skills were most needed to guide the Covenant of the League of Nations through the Senate, Wilson was unable to provide any leadership. The British ambassador who was sent over to help Wilson win acceptance for the League of Nations was not even received at the White House.

The Senate defeated Wilson's proposal that the United States accept the Covenant without any changes. All of Wilson's advisers from the Paris Peace Conference recommended that Wilson accept the League of Nations treaty with Lodge's reservations. Unwilling to compromise, Wilson urged his supporters to reject a motion that would have put the United States into the League of Nations under the conditions stated by Lodge. The Senate failed to get the needed two-thirds majority for the treaty.

Leaders of the victorious countries meet to determine the future of post-World War I Europe. From left, Vittorio Emanuele Orlando (1860-1952) of Italy, David Lloyd George (1863-1945) of Britain, Georges Clemenceau (1841-1929) of France, and Woodrow Wilson of the United States.

HINDSIGHT

Looking back on his failed effort to gain acceptance for the League of Nations in his own country, Wilson took a surprising view of the situation. "I think it best that the United States did not join the League of Nations. It might have been only a personal victory. Now when people join the League it will be because they are convinced it is the only right time for them to do it."

Unfortunately, there never was a "right time" for the League of Nations. The issue was never put to another vote. The United States never joined the League of Nations.

Wilson's fear of upcoming war proved to be justified. Without the participation of the United States, the League of Nations accomplished little. Twenty years following the end of the "war to end all wars," violence and hatred exploded into an even larger, more terrible world war. The horror of this war finally persuaded the United States not only to join, but also to be instrumental in establishing something similar to the League of Nations—the United Nations.

World War II was exactly what Wilson had feared and tried so hard to prevent. Whether the League of Nations could have prevented the war is debatable. But the failure of Wilson's strategy for winning the approval of the Senate meant that the League never got the chance to try.

The League of Nations continued to meet throughout the Second World War, accomplishing little until it quietly dissolved on April 19, 1946.

With his armies having conquered almost all of western Europe by mid-1940, Germany's Adolf Hitler seemed invincible.

3

ENTANGLING ALLIANCES
December 1940

You have watched with alarm as the rebuilt armies of Germany have swept across the continent of Europe. By late spring of 1940, Austria, Czechoslovakia, Poland, Belgium, the Netherlands, and France had all fallen. Since then, Great Britain has stood alone as the only nation opposing Germany in western Europe. The British government is pleading with you for help.

German leader Adolf Hitler is determined to make Germany a dominant world power and has shown that he will use force to get whatever he wants. For the time being, the Atlantic Ocean protects the United States from German aggression. But at the rate Hitler is seizing countries, the United States may one day find itself standing alone in the world against Germany and its allies.

Although Great Britain is in grave danger, the British are putting up a brave fight. Their outnumbered Royal Air Force pilots fought so well against the German air force during the summer that the Germans were forced to postpone a mass invasion of Great Britain. Despite the odds against them, the British believe that with a little help from the United States they can defeat the Germans. "Give us the tools and we will finish the job," says British Prime Minister Winston Churchill.

BACKGROUND

The situation, however, is not so simple. Great Britain is in danger. The German military is far stronger than theirs. Only the difficulty of launching an invasion across the English Channel has saved the British so far. The Germans have changed strategies for the moment and are now trying to bomb Great Britain into submission. Every night German bombers drop their deadly loads over British cities. Craters fill London's streets; fire-bombing has reduced many buildings to rubble.

Meanwhile, German warships and U-boats (submarines) prowl the shipping lanes, destroying Great Britain's desperately needed supplies. Controlling bases along the coast of Europe from Norway to France, the Germans can patrol a wide section of the Atlantic Ocean. In a period of five weeks ending in early November, they sank 400,000 tons of materials headed for Great Britain. If this continues, the British will soon lack the goods and equipment they need to survive.

Prime Minister Winston Churchill rallied the British people with inspiring speeches, but he knew that it would take more than words to defeat the Germans.

As Churchill has said, "The decision for '41 lies upon the seas." Great Britain urgently needs a large number of warships to protect and maintain its supply routes. Both your military and economic advisers agree that the United States has the industrial capacity to produce enough war supplies to arm Great Britain without weakening its own defenses. The problem is, how are the British going to pay for these supplies?

The war has been enormously costly for Great Britain. The additional cost of the supplies they will need to defend their colonies in Asia and North Africa against the Germans is staggering. Their government frankly admits that they cannot begin to pay for the supplies. Great Britain is asking you either to lend them the supplies or to give them the materials as an outright gift.

That puts you in a bind. According to the Neutrality Act passed by Congress in 1935, your government may not make loans to countries that are at war. As far as giving anything away, the hardworking citizens of your country may not take kindly to the suggestion that the United States spend billions of dollars for the defense of a foreign country.

Furthermore, the United States has long heeded the advice of Thomas Jefferson, who warned against getting caught up in "entangling alliances." Previous presidents have tried hard to avoid getting closely involved in European affairs. Even when the United States was finally pulled into the conflict of World War I, President Wilson referred to the United States as only an "Associate Power," not as an ally. The U.S. Senate rejected American involvement in the League of Nations out of this same fear of being forced to take military action because of commitments made to allies.

The events of the recent presidential campaign compound this reluctance to get involved in alliances. You had been coasting to victory until Wendell Wilkie, your challenger, discovered an issue that he could use against you. Wilkie predicted that if the American people elected you to another term, you would send American troops into battle in Europe.

The issue tapped deeply into American fears, and Wilkie's charge raised enough doubt in the minds of voters to reduce your comfortable lead in the polls. To reassure voters, in your final campaign speech you took a strong, unmistakable stand against direct American involvement in the wars of Europe. "I have said it before, but I shall say it again and again and again: your boys are not going to be sent into foreign wars." You ended up winning the election handily. But having made your vow, you must be careful about how involved you get with Great Britain's war, or you risk losing the public trust.

THE DECISION IS YOURS.

What are you going to do about Great Britain's desperate request for aid?

Option 1 **Do everything you can, short of war, to support Great Britain against Germany.**

Your support could be in the form of either loans or gifts or both. Secretary of War Henry Stimson and others in your administration have been advising you to choose

Though he doubted the British could hold out long against Germany, U.S. Secretary of War Henry Stimson (1867-1950) advised the president to honor Churchill's request for help.

this course. This is more than a case of sending aid to another country—this action is necessary to ensure the long-term survival of your country. The German war machine under the control of the Nazis may pose the greatest threat to democracy the world has ever known. Germany has demonstrated awesome military strength. Its blitzkrieg (lightning war) destroyed the Polish army in a matter of days. Even the armies of France, reputed to have been the strongest in the world, collapsed like dust cakes in the face of the German advance. A belief that they are the master race fuels the Nazi designs of world conquest.

Great Britain represents a buffer zone between you and the Nazis. If you are serious about staying out of war, then you had better maintain that buffer zone. That means doing all you can to support those who are now fighting the Nazis. You must ship Britain the supplies it needs. To guarantee that the supplies arrive safely, American warships must escort the ships.

If you do not lift a finger to support those standing against Germany, you are leading the United States down a dangerous road. The Nazis will probably continue to expand their empire until it laps at the shores of the United States. If the Germans then decide to attack North America, you will have no choice but to fight. By then, you would have no allies left to support you; the Nazis would have conquered all of them. Providing military equipment to Great Britain, whose defense would be vital to the defense of the United States, is a matter of self-defense.

This option could require some strong, possibly controversial, action from Congress. For one thing, Congress would need to repeal the Neutrality Act that it passed to calm American fears of getting entangled with warring European countries. Asking Congress to repeal the act may spark some controversy, but you have had great success in working with Congress. It has passed virtually every foreign policy measure that you have requested over the past few years.

This course of action could also run into some opposition from the general public, who might balk at footing the bill for the defense of Great Britain. On the other hand, public opinion polls have shown that even though Americans remain reluctant to get involved in foreign wars, they favor giving some kind of aid to Great Britain.

The most serious problem with *Option 1* is that if you get too enthusiastic about providing aid to Great Britain, you run a great risk of getting sucked into the European war you promised during the presidential campaign to avoid. Suppose you begin providing naval escorts for supply ships headed to Great Britain. As you explained to reporters on one occasion, "When a nation convoys ships there is apt to be some shooting, and shooting comes awfully close to war." In fact, this type of situation—German attacks on American ships headed for Germany's enemies—was what finally nudged the United States into World War I.

Generous aid to Great Britain also runs the risk of propelling you into the war by provoking Germany. You can hardly expect the Germans to consider the United States a neutral country if America is providing their enemy with the military equipment to kill German soldiers. By funneling massive aid to Great Britain you are, in effect, declaring war on Germany. Germany would be justified in fighting back.

German submarines roaming the Atlantic Ocean caused serious damage to Britain's shipping—and threatened to sink any ships that came to Britain's aid.

Option 2 **Work around loopholes in the Neutrality Act to aid Great Britain.**

A safer course of action might be a series of exchanges and leases between Great Britain and the United States. One type of policy under this option would be a "lend-lease" deal. This would involve sending military equipment to the British without charging them for it, with the understanding that Britain would return the equipment and make some kind of repayment after the war. Although this sounds like a loan, you could technically get around the Neutrality Act's ban on loans to warring countries by asking for repayment in something other than money.

For example, during the past year, Great Britain repeatedly asked for destroyers to help its navy deal with German submarines. You could not *give* the warships to Great Britain and still claim to be neutral. Moreover, the Neutrality Act prohibited you from lending the ships to the British for money to be repaid. But you found a way around that problem by giving the destroyers in exchange for the right to use some British military bases. Perhaps you could work out similar agreements on a larger scale for all the supplies you now want to send to Great Britain.

Eliminating the dollar sign gives you a number of advantages. For instance, you can get around the Neutrality Act without having to repeal it. Although you might get the law repealed, why take a chance? After all, the Senate Foreign Relations Committee that would hold hearings on the matter includes some of the strongest opponents of American foreign involvement: Hiram

Johnson of California and Robert La Follette, Jr., of Wisconsin. Look what happened to Woodrow Wilson when he tried to deal with those kinds of people on the League of Nations.

The lend-lease policy gives you flexibility in providing aid without blatantly taking Britain's side and giving up your neutrality. Repayment can be basically whatever you want it to be, so you can give the British some great bargains while appearing to make deals for your own business interests.

The down side of this approach is that it is at least partly a policy of deception. If you look at the policy closely, lend-lease makes poor business sense. It allows the United States to increase production of war goods primarily for Great Britain's use. This will be expensive for the U.S., which will get nothing in return for quite a while. Then, when the war is over and the material is no longer needed, the British will return it. What good will war material do the United States after the war is over?

The bottom line is that lend-lease is basically a scheme to arm Great Britain while getting around the law and pretending to stay neutral. Is giving presidents the power to do things unregulated by laws a wise choice?

Option 3 Go to war on Great Britain's side.

Why play this game of pretending to be neutral? You know what the Nazis are and what they are after. The world will know no peace as long as they remain in power.

Joining the war against Germany will take a great deal of courage, especially in view of your repeated campaign promise to keep Americans out of war. If you can expect opposition to a policy of openly supporting and arming Britain, the heat you will get for actually going to war will be even more fierce. But given the desperate stakes, you cannot afford to play it safe. As you have said, "Never before since Jamestown and Plymouth Rock has our American civilization been in such danger as now." You must take a chance and work hard to persuade people that Germany's policies make war inevitable anyway, so you might as well fight while you still have allies.

Option 4 **Turn down Great Britain's request.**

The American public has heard you proclaim loudly and emphatically that you would not send American soldiers to fight in Europe. They elected you with that understanding. If you break faith now, you lose the trust of the people at a crucial time.

The slogan "No Foreign Wars" still has a powerful hold on the American public. The European nations have been fighting for almost as long as anyone can remember, and they keep drawing the rest of the world into their fights. What good did American involvement in World War I do? The defeated Germans came back stronger and more vindictive than ever.

One of America's most popular heroes, aviator Charles Lindbergh, leads a determined group of people who oppose any sort of U.S. involvement in the war. They insist that the United States has no stake in the outcome of Europe's wars. By sending military supplies to Great Britain, the United States simply increases the likelihood that more people will be killed. Rather than becoming a part of the problem by adding to the violence,

Americans should be part of the solution and seek a negotiated end to the fighting.

Even if you believe that war with Germany is inevitable and that the United States should do all it can to support its allies against the Nazis, you still have a good reason to deny the British request for aid. General George Marshall, the army chief of staff, argues that the aid would come too late for Great Britain. Even if the U.S. arms them heavily, the British cannot hold out against the might of the Germans. The Germans will capture any equipment the United States sends to Britain. By arming Great Britain, the United States will then, in effect, be arming Germany, its most terrible enemy. When war with Germany comes, the Nazis will be using American equipment against Americans.

YOU ARE THE PRESIDENT. WHAT IS YOUR DECISION?

Option 1   **Do everything you can, short of war, to support Great Britain against Germany.**

Option 2   **Work around loopholes in the Neutrality Act to aid Great Britain.**

Option 3   **Go to war on Great Britain's side.**

Option 4   **Turn down Great Britain's request.**

*Could President Franklin D. Roosevelt (1882-1945)
help the British without defying Congress?*

President Franklin Roosevelt chose *Option 2*.

Roosevelt's campaign promise not to send Americans to fight in foreign wars had been so emphatic that he could hardly back down and send American troops to fight in Europe. He decided to use American military force only when the U.S. was directly threatened or attacked.

Roosevelt, in his state of the union speech (dubbed the "Four Freedoms" speech) on January 6, 1941, told the American people why they must support Britain: "No realistic American can expect from a dictator's peace international generosity, or return of true independence, or world disarmament, or freedom of expression, or freedom of religion—or even good business." Roosevelt believed that the Nazis wanted to conquer the world and that the best interests of the U.S. would be achieved by supporting any country fighting against Germany. He declared that the United States should be the "great arsenal of democracy." He accepted Churchill's argument that the British, if properly supplied, would hold off the Nazis and prevent American war materials from falling into German hands. That left Roosevelt debating how to lend this support to Britain. He wanted to find a way to accomplish this without tearing America apart or pulling it too quickly into war. According to an aide who accompanied Roosevelt on a Caribbean cruise in December 1940, "one evening he suddenly came out with it—the whole program."

Roosevelt publicly rejected the idea of repealing the Neutrality Act or giving arms to Great Britain. Instead, he asked Congress for sweeping powers to send war supplies to any country whose defense was in the interests of the United States and to arrange terms of sale, transfer, or lease.

RESULT

Roosevelt's proposals triggered an initial outcry of anger, especially from isolationists like Charles Lindbergh. Senator Burton Wheeler of Montana declared, "Never before has the United States given to one man the power to strip this nation of its defenses." For a brief time, the press engaged in a heated debate. The Chicago *Tribune* described Roosevelt's plan as "a bill for the destruction of the American Republic."

But in the end, Roosevelt used his political skill to win over the public and Congress. The House of Representative passed his program easily. The Senate, after a few modifications to which Roosevelt agreed, also passed the bill. Roosevelt signed it into law on March 11, 1941.

The Lend-Lease Act provided Great Britain with crucial aid that helped it survive the early months of 1941. Later that year, two events worked in favor of Roosevelt's decision. First, Germany invaded the Soviet Union in June. This eased the pressure on Great Britain, which had been fighting Germany by itself. Then in December, the Japanese, who were allies of Germany, launched an attack on the American naval base at Pearl Harbor, Hawaii. Congress responded by declaring war on Japan; Germany supported its ally by declaring war on the United States. The United States was now at war with Germany.

The public, aroused by the Japanese attack, overwhelmingly supported fighting alongside Great Britain against Germany. Roosevelt had accomplished his goal of helping Great Britain survive without leading the United States into an unpopular or controversial foreign war.

A poll taken two months after the passage of the Lend-Lease Act showed that half of the Americans polled believed that Roosevelt's program provided just the right amount of backing for Great Britain. About a fourth thought the program offered too much help; another fourth thought it offered too little. That balanced split showed Roosevelt had walked the tightrope of public opinion perfectly.

The powers that Roosevelt assumed under the Lend-Lease Act to make deals with Great Britain have alarmed some legal scholars. They have described his program as a sneaky way to wage war without asking Congress to declare it as required by law.

But, in a time of deadly peril, Roosevelt did achieve excellent results. Perhaps he could have accomplished as much with a more straightforward approach; perhaps not. At any rate, many experts believe that Roosevelt's decision to offer lend-lease aid to Great Britain marked a turning point in the war.

Only months after Lend-Lease, President Roosevelt asked Americans to enter the war.

4

To End the War
Summer 1945

On April 12, 1945, President Franklin Roosevelt died while in office. He left you, his vice-president, an awesome present. Three months after assuming your duties as president, you find yourself in charge of the most terrible weapon in the history of the world: the atomic bomb.

When the latest research indicated that an atomic bomb might be possible, a group of scientists set development of the bomb in motion. Frightened at the prospect of the brutal German government of Adolf Hitler being the first to wield such a powerful weapon, these scientists prodded Roosevelt into authorizing the enormously costly Manhattan Project to beat the Germans to the goal. While the United States fought alongside its allies in World War II against the Axis powers of Germany, Italy, and Japan, Roosevelt poured $2 billion into the project that involved thousands of workers over a three-and-a-half year period.

Fortunately, the Germans never came close to solving the problems involved in building an atomic bomb. The Allies defeated them shortly after you took office and ended the Nazi threat. By that time, however, the Manhattan Project was on the edge of achieving its mind-boggling goal. On July 16, 1945, American scientists successfully exploded an atomic bomb in the deserts of New Mexico. They measured the force of the blast as equal to 20,000 tons of TNT.

Now that you have the atomic bomb in your arsenal, your generals are urging you to use it.

BACKGROUND

The completion of the Manhattan Project may have come at a very opportune time. Although the Allied forces have defeated Germany and Italy, the United States and its allies are still at war with Japan. The tide of battle has turned overwhelmingly against the Japanese. The war has so devastated Japan's industries and military that it has virtually no hope of staving off a complete Allied victory. Yet, the Japanese have shown no intention of surrendering.

As commander-in-chief of the armed forces of the United States, your job is to decide the best way to get Japan to surrender. Given the fierce devotion of the Japanese to their country, an outright invasion of Japan is likely to be a long and bloody operation. You could keep American soldiers out of the line of fire by destroying

Japanese cities with conventional bombs and by blockading their ports until you break their will to fight. But, again, the Japanese disdain for surrendering means this could be a long, hideous campaign that would rain death down upon perhaps millions of Japanese civilians, including children.

The grim consequences of either—an outright invasion or bombing and blockading—lead to your consideration of the newly developed atomic bomb as a possible alternative. The power of this weapon is almost unimaginable. Perhaps a demonstration of its power would shock the Japanese into conceding that further resistance is utterly senseless.

THE DECISION IS YOURS.

What course of action will you take to force the Japanese to surrender?

Option 1 Invade Japan.

The traditional military approach to forcing the surrender of an enemy military force is to invade their territory, defeat their armies, and conquer their land. This is the most honorable method because it largely confines the killing to trained soldiers and spares innocent civilians.

Your generals have drawn up plans for an invasion of Japan. More than a million American soldiers will take part in the invasion. The schedule calls for an attack on the southern island of Kyushu in October 1945, followed by an invasion of the main Japanese island of Honshu in March 1946. Massive bombing against the Japanese defensive positions will support both attacks. In fact, the United States military is stockpiling more bombs for the pre-invasion bombardment of Japan than were dropped on Germany during the entire war.

Even with such powerful support, however, military experts predict that American casualties will be severe. The closer Allied troops have drawn to the Japanese home islands, the more fierce the fighting has become. Earlier this year, more than 4,000 American marines died capturing the tiny island of Iwo Jima. That was followed by over 12,000 American dead and 36,000 wounded in the battle for Okinawa, an island nearly 400 miles from the main Japanese islands. More than 100,000 Japanese soldiers and a similar number of civilians lost their lives defending Okinawa.

Japan will have at least 20 times more soldiers defending the main islands than they had on Okinawa. Some of its military leaders are itching for one last chance to uphold their honor as fighting men. They will fight fanatically. Most observers expect the invasion to be the bloodiest assault of the war. Estimates for casualties that American troops will sustain range from 250,000 upward. Japanese casualties will likely be far greater.

Option 2 Bomb and blockade.

Bombing and blockading are twin methods of weakening an enemy's resolve. While blockading enemy ports to starve the opposing forces of supplies has been a traditional military strategy, the bombing of cities is something new. At the start of World War II, most nations considered the bombing of a city to be a despicable war crime.

But this war has changed all that. German planes bombed Warsaw in the early fighting of 1939. The British began bombing German cities in 1940, and the Germans upped the ante with a devastating bombing campaign against London. Although these attacks were primarily aimed at destroying industry, the bombings slaughtered civilians by the thousands. In February 1945, British and American air raids on the German city of Dresden set off an inferno that killed at least 35,000 people.

The bombing missions of your air force on Japan have been even more destructive. Unfortunately, Japanese factories are not concentrated in specific industrial areas within each city. Rather, the factories are scattered about the city and surrounded by the living quarters of the factory workers. This means that precise bombing of military targets without killing civilians is nearly impossible.

On the night of March 9, 1945, a bombing raid lasting just 30 minutes dropped more than 1,000 tons of incendiary bombs on Tokyo, killing over 83,000 Japanese, injuring another 41,000, and completely destroying 15.8 square miles of the city. In the past few months, similar attacks on Nagoya, Osaka, Kobe, and another on Tokyo killed thousands more civilians.

Despite the horrible losses these raids have inflicted on the Japanese, they have not produced any noticeable weakening in the country's determination to fight on. A continuation of this type of bombing may exact an enormous toll of death and destruction before it forces a surrender. The American public, bitter at the Japanese sneak attack on Pearl Harbor at the start of the war and at

Waves of American B-29s drop tons of incendiary bombs on Yokohama, Japan, wrecking almost seven square miles of the city.

reports of atrocities committed by Japanese forces, has little sympathy for Japan. Nevertheless, a continued wholesale slaughter of civilians might well repulse the American public. Further, much of the world has been at war for six years, and your own country has been fighting for more than three years. Americans are tired of war. Neither bombing raids nor blockades will end the war quickly, if at all.

Option 3 **Demonstrate the power of your atomic bombs in an effort to persuade the Japanese to surrender.**

You now have an awesome weapon that cost your country a fortune to develop. This may be the perfect time to use it. When the Japanese see that you have the power to obliterate an entire city with a single bomb, they will recognize that they have no choice but to stop fighting. If this strategy works, you will stop the war, save the lives of thousands of American soldiers, and avoid the shaky moral position of killing hundreds of thousands of civilians.

You can accomplish this demonstration in two ways. One way would be to drop the bomb on an unpopulated location. By so doing, you would demonstrate the bomb's power without harming anyone.

Most of your advisers, however, believe that the Japanese will not be impressed unless they see and feel the terrifying destruction that the bomb is capable of. If a bombing raid that killed over 80,000 people and injured 40,000 more did not intimidate the Japanese, how likely are they to be cowed by a harmless exhibition? Most of your advisers believe that there is no way to arrange a demonstration that would provide the kind of shock that would force the Japanese to surrender.

Furthermore, your scientists have not been able to mass-produce the uranium and plutonium needed for the bombs. At the moment, you have only two atomic bombs in your arsenal, and building more could take some time. If you use one in a harmless demonstration that does not bring about surrender, you've wasted half your atomic capability.

An alternate method of demonstration would be to drop a bomb on an industrial city in Japan but to warn the people ahead of time so they would leave the city. That would provide the spectacular destruction needed to shock the Japanese and force them to see reason without causing a tremendous loss of life. Your advisers point out a number of concerns with this option. The atomic bomb has never been tested under war conditions. What if your demonstration does not work? The fiasco might boost the enemy's spirits and actually prolong the war.

In addition, how do you warn the Japanese away from a target without exposing your bombers to risk? If the enemy knows when and where to expect the attack, your bombers will be sitting ducks for antiaircraft fire. The possibility also exists that the Japanese would move American prisoners of war into the target areas.

Option 4 **Drop atomic bombs on selected Japanese industrial cities.**

Before American scientists even tested the first bomb, a joint panel of scientific and military experts had recommended that you use the new bombs as soon as they were ready.

This may seem cruel. As mentioned before, Japanese industrial targets are often located among civilian centers

Atomic bombs nicknamed Little Boy . . .

and so your bombs would kill great numbers of civilians. But one or two devastating explosions is far more likely to shock Japan into surrendering than a mere demonstration would. Like *Option 3,* this would spare American and Japanese soldiers from a bloody battle for Japan and spare Japanese citizens a prolonged bombing campaign. *Option 4* simply has a greater chance of succeeding. Great Britain's leader, Winston Churchill, believes you should use your atomic bombs without hesitation. Most of your advisers agree.

Your country has invested a great deal of money and effort into developing this military advantage. Can you, in good conscience, send American soldiers into battle without providing them the greatest amount of firepower at your command?

The disadvantage with this option is that you would be ushering into the world an entirely new weapon—one that could threaten the survival of the planet. One of

. . . and Fat Man

the engineers who worked on the Manhattan Project warned that using this bomb would set off a dangerous nuclear arms race among the nations. "As horrible as it may seem," he wrote, "I know it would be better to take greater casualties now in conquering Japan than to bring upon the world the tragedy of unrestrained competitive production of this material."

These doubts are not restricted to scientists. General Dwight Eisenhower, the commander of the Allied forces that overwhelmed Germany's western front, believes that Japan's position is already so hopeless that drastic action is not required, and he hopes that the United States is not the first to use such a horrible weapon. If you do use the bomb, history will remember you as the one who escalated war into the atomic age and who did so against innocent civilians, including children.

YOU ARE THE PRESIDENT.
WHAT IS YOUR DECISION?

Option 1   Invade Japan.

Option 2   Bomb and blockade.

Option 3   Demonstrate the power of your atomic bombs in an effort to persuade the Japanese to surrender.

Option 4   Drop atomic bombs on selected Japanese industrial cities.

President Harry Truman (1884-1972) was the first leader in history to have the atomic bomb at his disposal.

President Harry Truman chose *Option 4*.

Writing in his diary in the weeks before the bomb was dropped, Truman admitted, "I do not like the weapon." But after long and careful thought, he reluctantly agreed with the majority of his advisers who urged him to use the atomic bomb against Japan. Perhaps the best insight into his thinking at the time was a comment that he made in private: "Think of the kids who won't be killed." As one who had fought in the trenches during World War I, Truman was especially eager to spare American soldiers the ordeal of a brutal last battle for Japan.

Some historians have suggested that the military was so strongly in favor of using the atomic bomb that Truman had no choice. According to one, "Had Truman refused to go ahead, he might well have been impeached." Truman, however, always accepted the decision as his own. He was not one to be hesitant about making decisions, nor did he spend time worrying about what critics would think of his choices. "If the facts available justify a decision at the time, it will also be correct in future time," he said.

On July 26, 1945, Truman authorized the U. S. military to use the atomic bomb on the condition that it wait until he returned home from a meeting in Europe. Truman's conference ended on August 2.

RESULT

On August 6, the U.S. bomber *Enola Gay* flew toward the city of Hiroshima. The American commanders selected this target because it was the southern headquarters and supply depot for Japan's homeland army.

American pilots had dropped warning leaflets more than a week earlier. But these had not been specific about what was to come. They merely promised "prompt and utter" destruction if the Japanese did not surrender—a typical wartime boast.

At 8:15 A.M. Hiroshima time, the *Enola Gay* dropped a single bomb, *Little Boy*, on Hiroshima. The explosion was even more devastating than the Americans expected. It instantly leveled over 60 percent of the city. The firestorm unleashed by the bomb burned to ash all buildings within a half mile of the blast. More than 70,000 occupants of the city died in a searing flash of heat. A few days later, on August 9, at 11:01 A.M., the United States dropped a second bomb, *Fat Man*, from the bomber *Bock's Car* on the city of Nagasaki, killing an estimated 20,000 people.

Hiroshima shows the effects of the first atomic bomb.

A gigantic mushroom cloud looms over Nagasaki moments after the detonation of the second atomic bomb.

The two bombs provided the desired shock value. Japan surrendered on August 14, 1945. No invasion or further bombing was necessary.

The ruins of Nagasaki, one month after the great explosion

HINDSIGHT

Immediate reaction in the United States was favorable, especially among soldiers and their loved ones. The revulsion against the Japanese atrocities that were reported during the war hardened many Americans against feeling any sympathy for the victims of the blast.

Two nagging questions, however, remain unanswered to this day. Could the same result have been achieved by simply demonstrating what atomic weapons could do? If so, then Truman needlessly killed hundreds of thousands of people, including children. The question can never be answered. The results of actions not taken remain forever a mystery.

Second, was the immediate victory worth the long-range cost to both the United States and the world? One newspaper critic saw the danger immediately after the first bomb was dropped. "Yesterday we clinched victory in the Pacific," he wrote, "but we sowed the whirlwind."

As one of the long-range effects of that whirlwind, many people around the world, including some Americans, view the bombing of Hiroshima as a blot on the honor of the United States. How has that affected American actions and how has that affected U.S. relations with other countries? And what role did the decision to drop the atomic bomb play in triggering a nuclear arms race between the United States and the Soviet Union that cost billions of dollars, produced deadly radioactive waste, and created arsenals powerful enough to destroy the world many times over? Again, we can only speculate.

President Truman did not believe in second-guessing decisions and had little patience with those who tried. Until his death, Truman insisted that the bombs dropped on Hiroshima and Nagasaki saved the lives of at least a quarter of a million American soldiers and far more Japanese soldiers and civilians. In a typically terse explanation of his decision, he once said, "I was there. I did it. I would do it again."

5

RACE RIOT
IN LITTLE ROCK
September 1957

Three years ago, on May 17, 1954, in the famous *Brown v. The Board of Education of Topeka* case, the Supreme Court unanimously declared segregated public school systems (those that enforced separate facilities for black and white students) illegal. The "separate but equal" rule of law that had stood as the foundation of segregation had been exposed as a fraud that violated the Fourteenth Amendment to the Constitution. Not only were separate facilities for blacks decidedly unequal, but the very existence of segregation laws also implied that black people were inferior.

This decision stirred up fires of resentment, especially in the South, where many whites did not want their children mixing with black children. Senator James Eastland of Mississippi symbolized the defiance of white southerners when he said that the South "will not abide by or obey this legislative decision by a political court." Aware that the roots of racial discrimination run deep in the South, you have advised patience and caution in dealing with this issue. The federal courts have taken your advice. Rather than set a timetable for integration, they have simply required that local school districts that currently segregate work toward a change in their policies.

While this lenient approach has avoided conflict for the most part, it has done so at the expense of racial progress. Most southern school boards have virtually ignored the Supreme Court's decision. By the end of the 1956-57 school year, no school integration had taken place in Alabama, Florida, Georgia, Louisiana, Mississippi, North Carolina, South Carolina, and Virginia.

As chairman of the Senate Judiciary Committee, staunch segregationist James Eastland, who represented Mississippi from 1941 to 1979, greatly hindered the creation of civil rights laws.

But now the lid that you have tried to maintain on the simmering passions over racial justice is threatening to blow off. An attempt to desegregate Central High School in the Arkansas capital of Little Rock has triggered the kind of crisis you have desperately been hoping to avoid.

BACKGROUND

Ironically, the crisis has developed in Arkansas, one of the few southern states that has made some effort to achieve school integration. Nine years ago, Arkansas became the first former Confederate state to open its state universities to black students. The Little Rock school board was among the first southern school boards to develop a definite schedule for integrating its public schools. Shortly after the *Brown* verdict, the board produced plans for integrating its high schools in 1957, its junior highs in 1960, and its elementary schools in 1963.

Right on schedule, eight black students enrolled at Central High School for the 1957 school year. This was more than local segregationists could stand. Led by the Mother's League of Little Rock, they took legal steps to keep blacks out of their schools by filing suit in Pulaski County Court on August 28, 1957. On August 29, the court granted the segregationists a temporary injunction ordering the school board to halt the integration of Central High. School officials responded by appealing to the federal courts. Federal Judge Ronald Davies promptly overruled the county court and ordered the integration to proceed as planned. Segregationists called on Arkansas Governor Orval Faubus for help.

On September 2, Faubus ordered the Arkansas National Guard to Central High School to prevent the entry of any black students. On September 4, under orders from Faubus, these guardsmen defied the federal court by turning away the black students who attempted to enter the school.

Those in favor of integrating the schools demanded that the federal government enforce the law. At the same time, segregationists stepped up their efforts against integration. Brushfires of racial violence flared up in Little Rock and showed signs of igniting in other areas of the South. On September 9, a newly integrated school in Nashville, Tennessee, was dynamited.

Initially, you tried to stay out of the dispute. But in an attempt to quell the growing disturbance, you met with Governor Faubus. Following a long discussion with him, you thought the two of you had come to an understanding. You assured the governor that you would not call federal troops into the crisis, and he indicated he would obey the court order and allow the black students to enter the school. But when Faubus returned to Arkansas, he continued to use the National Guard to deny the black pupils' entry.

Mounting pressure from the federal courts quickly forced Faubus to change tactics. He ordered the National Guard to leave Central High School. Now the black students were free to enter the school. A couple of weeks ago, this action might have had a chance of defusing the situation. But by this time, racial tensions had reached the boiling point. With the schoolyard unpatrolled by either the National Guard or local police, black students had to attend the high school at their own risk.

Arkansas Governor Orval Faubus

On September 23, eight black students quietly walked into Central High through a side door. Word of this entry quickly leaked out to the community. Soon an angry mob, possibly numbering in the thousands and including an aide of Governor Faubus, surrounded the school and demanded that the black students leave. In the ugly scene that followed, a shouting mob spat on and abused the departing blacks. You issued a statement condemning the actions of the mob and made a plea for the people's "sense of justice and fair play" to quiet the situation.

But today the mob has come back—larger and angrier. Violence has escalated. You have just received a frantic call from Woodrow Wilson Mann, the mayor of Little Rock. Declaring the situation "out of control," Mann has asked for federal troops to help restore order. What will you do?

THE DECISION IS YOURS.

How will you respond to the deteriorating situation in Little Rock?

Option 1 **Respect states' rights and stay out.**

The immediate situation is not a problem involving the national government; it is a problem involving the city of Little Rock and the state of Arkansas. You have clearly stated many times during your administration that you do not intend to interfere with the rights of states to handle their own affairs, including matters of racial equality. Last year, when authorities in Mansfield, Texas, turned away black students trying to enter their schools, you did not get involved. Just two months ago, you stated that you could not "imagine any set of circumstances that would ever induce me to send federal troops . . . into any area to enforce the orders of a federal court, because I believe that common sense in America will never require it."

This is not simply a matter of supporting or opposing integrated schools. You have to guard against the possibility that heavy-handed action by the federal government could produce a terrible backlash from people who believe strongly in the rights of states to govern themselves without federal interference. You had anticipated a situation like this might occur, and you declared that "federal law imposed upon our states in such a way as to bring about a conflict of the police power of the state and the nation would set back the cause of progress in race relations for a long time."

The issue of the rights of states versus the power of the federal government is especially explosive in the South, which fought the Civil War over the very issue of states' rights. No matter how grave the situation in Little Rock, the act of sending federal troops into a southern state is likely to rip open the scars from that era. Many white southerners are still bitter over the memory of the northern troops stationed in the South following the war. The soldiers were associated with the northern "carpetbaggers"—northern politicians who, in the minds of white southerners, arrogantly mistreated and exploited the defeated South. The return of federal troops to enforce a locally unpopular school integration law will surely rekindle old hatreds. Increased violence and less tolerance and understanding among the races may result.

If your troops are put in a position in which they have to use force against civilians, this could touch off worse violence. The race issue is explosive with emotions close to the surface. The image of a fellow white southerner bleeding and dying at the hands of federal troops would inflame these emotions and provide segregationists with a powerful recruiting tool for their cause. The last thing you want is to provide the segregationists with martyrs and a reason to seek revenge.

If you need reminding of how deep the resentment of the post–Civil War occupation runs, you need only look at the political scorecard. The Republicans were the party in control of the nation at the time of the southern occupation. Ever since then, the South has voted Democratic in almost all elections. Some signs indicate that this trend may have changed in recent years. But you can expect white southerners to take out their resentment at the ballot box if you are not careful. You can't afford to inflame the hatred of the South against you if your party is to have any hope of winning national elections.

Finally, if you try to force people to do something they don't want to do, they will simply look for ways to get around your orders. A strong possibility exists that, rather than give in to aggressive enforcement of the Supreme Court decision on public school integration, the South will dismantle its entire public education system. This would leave only private schools, which the Supreme Court ruling does not cover. In that case, only wealthy whites would be able to afford good private schools for their children. Poor whites and blacks would be worse off than they are now.

All these reasons indicate that you would be better off letting the local officials handle their own problems.

Option 2 Work out a behind-the-scenes compromise with the officials of Little Rock and Arkansas.

The crisis in Little Rock is not an isolated problem. Racial tensions are high all over the South. If you don't find some way to deal with the crisis now, chaos and violence could easily escalate until the whole South is in an uproar.

Furthermore, this is not merely a local government matter. The segregationists are violating federal laws and federal court orders. As president of the United States, you have sworn that you will protect and defend the Constitution of the United States. If you just sit back and let people ignore the law, you are violating your oath.

On the other hand, advisers have constantly reminded you that the best way to win hearts and change minds is not through laws or force, but by persuasion. You have said yourself that "success through conciliation will be more lasting and stronger than could be obtained through force and conflict." The majority of public opinion favors your approach of caution and patience in the matter of school integration. Polls have shown that Americans support gradual desegregation.

Therefore, if you want to uphold your oath of office and the laws of the country yet stick to your course of patience and reason, you will work with the officials of Arkansas and Little Rock to find some sort of peaceful compromise that will end the crisis.

But can the voices of patience and reason make a difference at this stage? Mayor Mann sounds desperate. The situation is out of control. What happens if people are hurt and killed and if Little Rock is trashed while you sit back and negotiate with segregationists? How long are you willing to let a mob rampage through the streets while you seek some moderate compromise?

Furthermore, what has this policy of caution and patience accomplished? A strong case can be made that gentle persuasion is not working, that segregationists are simply taking advantage of you. Despite your moderate attempts to steer the South down a gradual course toward racial justice, the South has constructed more racial barriers than they have broken down. Since the *Brown* verdict, white-dominated southern legislatures have passed 130 laws supporting the segregation of races.

What did your attempts to reason with Governor Faubus accomplish? You tried to work out a solution to the problem with Faubus and thought you had succeeded. Then he backslid on the whole agreement and put you in a worse position than when you started.

Option 3 Send federal troops to Little Rock.

You have some compelling reasons to take decisive action despite the arguments made under *Option 1.* The situation in Little Rock is destroying your moral authority around the world. Just as you are trying to gather world opinion against the Soviets for their brutal invasion of Hungary, the Soviets are pointing to Little Rock as proof that Americans are hypocrites. The Soviets say that the United States sounds very eloquent in speaking for the rights of the Hungarian dissidents while at the same time oppressing minority groups in its own country.

More than a century ago, the actions of President Andrew Jackson demonstrated another danger with the lax enforcement of federal laws. When a Supreme Court ruling struck down a Georgia law dealing with American Indian policy in 1832, the government of Georgia refused to obey the decision. President Jackson, who also disliked the decision, refused to enforce it.

This action encouraged states to be even more aggressive about asserting their rights. South Carolina even declared its right to disregard any federal law it did not like. Jackson came to realize that the nation could not be held together unless the states respected federal laws. He put a stop to the states' bold declarations of independence by declaring he would bring force against any state that refused to obey federal laws.

By not firmly enforcing federal laws, you run the same risk that Jackson did of losing control of the country. You have insisted that you intend to "uphold the constitutional process in this country." Now would be a good time to prove that.

Finally, this is not strictly a matter of the federal government overriding the rights of states. This is not an action that you have decided to take on your own. The mayor of Little Rock has asked you to send troops. Mayor Mann does not want to see federal troops in his city if their presence can be avoided. He never would have made such a drastic request unless he was at the end of his rope. The situation is dangerously out of control. A mob is threatening the well-being of citizens who are granted equal protection under the law. You need to take action immediately.

YOU ARE THE PRESIDENT. WHAT IS YOUR DECISION?

Option 1	Respect states' rights and stay out.
Option 2	Work out a behind-the-scenes compromise with the officials of Little Rock and Arkansas.
Option 3	Send federal troops to Little Rock.

President Dwight Eisenhower (1890-1969) had to weigh political considerations, including the future of the Republican party in the South, with the responsibility of carrying out the Supreme Court's Brown v. Board of Education *decision.*

President Dwight Eisenhower chose *Option 3*.

This action went against Eisenhower's nature and his philosophy. In the area of civil rights, Eisenhower had a reputation for moving cautiously in steering what he called "a difficult course between extremist firebrands and extremist diehards." After Supreme Court Chief Justice Earl Warren produced the *Brown* verdict that ruled segregated schools to be a violation of federal law, Eisenhower regretted his appointment of Warren to the Court, calling it the worst decision he had ever made. Eisenhower preferred to appeal to people's reason and fairness. He was so eager to find compromises that political rival Adlai Stevenson called Eisenhower "a man infatuated with the idea of compromise as a solution for everything."

In this case, however, compromise did not seem to be an option. The mob in Little Rock had degenerated beyond the reach of reason. Furthermore, Eisenhower felt that segregationists, particularly Governor Faubus, had betrayed him by taking advantage of his moderate stance. Eisenhower knew that trust is a necessary element in compromise. The president, angered by what he called Faubus's "stupidity and duplicity," certainly did not trust the governor anymore.

That left Eisenhower with the choice of either going in or staying out. He had made it clear, particularly in Texas, that he would go to great lengths to avoid involving the federal government in state issues. But this time, the level of violence caused him to change his mind and to do his duty to protect and defend the Constitution. Under Eisenhower's orders, federal soldiers were sent to the

South to protect the rights of blacks for the first time since the post–Civil War Reconstruction. Still uncomfortable with interfering in the affairs of local school boards, Eisenhower explained that he had decided to send in federal troops "not to compel integration but to uphold the rule of law versus mob rule."

Eisenhower immediately placed the Arkansas National Guard under federal command. These soldiers were quickly reinforced by 1,000 paratroopers who flew into Little Rock that night.

President Eisenhower signs the order authorizing the use of federal troops to desegregate Little Rock's public schools.

White students watch as federal troops escort black students into Little Rock's Central High School.

RESULT

By the morning of September 25, the grounds around Central High School were secure. That morning, federal troops escorted nine black students to the school without major incident.

Sporadic violence broke out in isolated cases, and the black students remained under the protection of the soldiers for several months. But the segregationists' protest had lost its steam, and the crisis died down. As the streets quieted, Eisenhower gradually removed troops. Within two years, Little Rock's Central High School had achieved its goal of peaceful integration.

Southern politicians bitterly criticized Eisenhower's actions. Senator Richard Russell of Georgia called the move illegal and compared the federal troops to Hitler's storm troopers. Arkansas did try to carry out its threat to dissolve the state educational system and support a new private school system. The attempt failed, however, when the federal courts declared that a state government could not legally fund a private school system.

Despite the success of his policy in Little Rock, Eisenhower remained uncomfortable with the idea of involving the federal government in the civil rights issues of any state. Never again did he take firm action to enforce a federal court decision. His policy of gentle persuasion produced few results in the rest of his administration. By 1959, more than 70 percent of the white South still disagreed with the school desegregation ruling.

Eisenhower's use of troops in this situation was widely hailed as the proper decision. Opinion polls taken soon after the crisis showed that nearly two-thirds of all Americans agreed with Eisenhower's action. Black leaders such as Martin Luther King, Jr., who had been impatient with Eisenhower's slow reforms, supported the decision. So did more than a third of white southerners.

As an added bonus for Eisenhower, his action did not permanently alienate the South from his Republican party. In fact, within a decade, the South was well on its way to becoming a Republican presidential stronghold.

6

THE NUCLEAR EDGE
October 1962

Cuba has been a thorn in your side ever since you took office. This island nation off the coast of Florida has become firmly allied with your greatest enemy, the Soviet Union. Many Americans are uneasy about having a Communist country so near to their border. As a result, the United States has continued efforts to destabilize the Communist government of Cuba.

Since mid-August, an unusually large number of Soviet ships have docked in Cuban harbors. To prevent you from observing them, the Cubans and Soviets unloaded many of the ships at night. On August 20, John McCone, your CIA director, told you that he had information that Cuba was building nuclear missile sites. You and your staff have been hesitant to believe him because he is a fanatical anti-Communist. For the Soviets to threaten the United States in such a way when the U.S. holds such an overwhelming advantage in nuclear weapons makes no sense. On August 29, you did obtain aerial photos of Soviet-built antiaircraft missile sites in Cuba. This upset you, but you can accept the antiaircraft missiles because they are strictly defensive in nature.

Since August, though, tensions have been slowly rising, and the American public has become more and more uncomfortable with having Communists in their back yard. In an effort to find out what was going on, your intelligence units took new aerial photographs of Cuba on October 14, 1962. They enlarged and studied miles of film. As you view the evidence today, you no longer have any doubt as to what the Soviets are doing. The photographs have detected at least nine Soviet missile sites under construction—many of them close to completion.

Aerial photographs such as this convinced the president that Soviet missiles in Cuba threatened U.S. security.

BACKGROUND

Without any missile bases in Cuba, the Soviet Union has very little "first strike" capability. In other words, even if they suddenly launched all their missiles at the U.S., the surprise attack would not erase American military superiority. The Soviet missiles are located in the Soviet Union—so far away that the United States would have plenty of time to respond before they arrived.

Missiles launched from Cuba, however, would be a different story. They could strike with so little warning that they could destroy nearly half the American bomber force before it got off the ground. These medium-range missiles are also more accurate than the long-range Soviet-based missiles.

Cuban missiles pose a serious threat to American civilians. According to intelligence reports, Soviet medium-range missile sites have been nearly completed. With a range of 1,200 miles, they could reach many American population centers in minutes. You estimate that Soviet intermediate-range missile sites will be in operation in Cuba by Christmas. The 2,200-mile range of these missiles would put Soviet nuclear bombs within minutes of every major mainland city in the United States, except for Seattle. With so little time to respond, these cities would be helpless against an attack. Cuban-based nuclear weapons would also threaten all the smaller countries in the Western hemisphere.

As of this moment, you do not know if the Soviets actually have nuclear warheads in Cuba. (Missiles are not dangerous in themselves—they are simply transportation devices. The warheads on the missiles contain the explosive.) Your intelligence agency has confirmed the presence of missiles, launch sites, and storage facilities, but not the actual warheads. However, you now know how well the Soviets can hide materials they want kept secret. Any decision you make must take into account the possibility that nuclear warheads are in Cuba, ready for action.

While you are not certain just what the Soviets have delivered to Cuba, you do have a good idea of what they have on the way. Your sources report seeing nuclear warheads loaded on a freighter at the Soviet city of Odessa. This freighter is on its way to Cuba, along with two dozen other ships belonging to the Soviet Union or its allies.

Yet despite the threat posed by these Cuban missile bases, the Soviets can present sound, nonthreatening reasons for building them. Your administration has made no secret of the fact that it would like to topple Fidel Castro's Communist government. Little more than a year has passed since an army of Cuban refugees, backed by the American government, launched an attack on Cuba. This halfhearted invasion attempt, crushed by the Cubans at the Bay of Pigs, brought shame to your administration, but it has not stopped you from supporting Cuban exiles in attacks against Cuba or making thinly veiled threats of invading Cuba. Given this conduct, the Cubans have reason to fear further action on the part of the United States, and their desire for Soviet missiles to protect them from a possible attack is understandable.

Second, your government has the Soviets at a huge disadvantage with regard to nuclear weapons, a point you have made repeatedly in public. The Soviets believe the mismatch makes them a tempting target for American aggression, and they are extremely nervous about being in this position. This increases the chances that they could panic, shoot first, and ask questions later. By strengthening their hand in Cuba, the Soviets are increasing world security as well as their own. Not only will the Cuban missiles make the United States think harder about going to war with the Soviets, but the security they provide will also make the Soviets less likely to make rash decisions.

Finally, in building missile bases in Cuba, the Soviets are doing exactly what the Americans have already done in Turkey. The U.S. has already installed offensive nuclear weapons on Turkish soil near the Soviet border, and they have aimed these missiles directly at the Soviet heartland. Is this any different from having Soviet missiles in Cuba?

THE DECISION IS YOURS.

Will you allow the missile bases to stay? If not, how will you get them out?

Option 1 Invade Cuba.

In a speech made last month, you publicly warned the Soviet Union not to put missiles in Cuba. They installed them anyway. If you let the Soviets get away with installing the missiles, you could lose credibility among world leaders, and the Soviets may conclude that you have no backbone. If they think they can push you around, who knows what aggressive actions they will take next?

You can justify military action by the fact that every nation has the right to defend its security. The Soviets are the aggressors in this case. While the act of installing deadly weapons along the American border is not a direct act of war, it is an aggressive action against the U.S.

Your military advisers tell you this is the perfect time and place to teach the Soviets a lesson. The Soviets have chosen a poor spot to confront the United States. Cuba is in America's back yard—within easy reach of U.S. soldiers and supplies. If the Soviets want to fight here, they will have to send troops and equipment from halfway around the world.

According to General Maxwell Taylor, your military situation is unbeatable. American forces would overwhelm Cuba long before help from the Soviet Union could arrive. The U. S. Army has put together the largest invasion force since World War II. More than 100,000 soldiers are posted in the southeastern United States, and thousands more marines are ready to go.

Although the Soviets could respond with nuclear weapons, it would be suicide for them to do so. The United States has roughly 5,000 nuclear weapons; you estimate the Soviet total at around 75. At this moment, 90 B-52 bombers are cruising over the Atlantic Ocean carrying nuclear bombs. For additional nuclear firepower, you can tap more than 500 additional bombers that stand in reserve on the ground and more than 150 land-based missiles. Several aircraft carriers and Polaris submarines are loaded with hundreds more nuclear weapons. All this is more than enough to annihilate the Soviet Union.

Even though you hold unquestioned military superiority, an invasion of Cuba would not be easy. The Central Intelligence Agency estimates that, in addition

At this White House meeting in October 1962, the president and his advisers discuss the threat posed by missiles in Cuba.

to the Cuban army, between 10,000 and 17,000 Soviet soldiers are stationed on the island. These troops may or may not have nuclear weapons available to them. If the Soviet troops do, and if they are put in a desperate situation, as is likely, individual commanders may be tempted to use these weapons, regardless of the orders of Soviet leaders in Moscow. In any case, an attack on Cuba will bring strong pressure on Soviet leader Nikita Khrushchev to retaliate in some way.

Option 2 Bomb the missile sites.

While your military advisers believe the U.S. should eventually invade Cuba, initially they favor bombing the missile sites.

Option 2 offers the advantage of a strong military response to the Soviets with fewer risks and fewer casualties than could be expected with *Option 1.* A bombing strike would show the Soviets that they cannot intimidate you, yet a strike would be less likely to escalate into a widespread war and would not put thousands of American soldiers in the line of fire. Aircraft could strike with little warning and clear out before the enemy could respond.

Time is also a key factor. Every day you wait puts the Soviets that much closer to having a powerful battery of nuclear missiles installed in Cuba and ready to fire. You could launch a bombing raid today with far less preparation than would be needed for an invasion.

On the minus side, the U.S. would be launching a surprise attack much like Japan did against Pearl Harbor. Doing so would cause the world to question the morality of the U.S. Militarily, air strikes are not as thorough as an invasion, so a certain amount of dangerous Soviet weaponry is likely to escape damage, no matter how thoroughly you bomb Cuba.

Air strikes against the missile sites also present some of the same dangers as *Option 1.* While less provoking than an invasion, a strike does not give the Soviets an "out." Therefore, they will feel strong pressure to retaliate to defend their honor.

Your generals cannot guarantee that an air strike will totally eliminate the Soviet nuclear threat. Although not likely, the Soviets might be able to launch nuclear missiles at U.S. cities even as the Cuban missile sites are being bombed. In fact, Soviet commanders under attack may be forced into a "use it or lose it" situation that causes them to fire their missiles. Soviet nuclear warheads are far more devastating than the atomic bombs that the United States used to destroy the Japanese cities of Hiroshima and Nagasaki in World War II. A single Soviet warhead exploding over an American city could kill or injure 5 million people.

Your secretary of defense, Robert McNamara, warns, "It is impossible to predict with a high degree of confidence what the effects of the use of military force will be because of the risks of accident, miscalculation, misperception, and inadvertence." When bullets are flying and bombs are dropping, the odds greatly increase that a misunderstanding on the part of either the Soviets or the Americans will escalate into a nuclear exchange. Any nuclear exchange, however limited, will cause horrible destruction in the United States. And the fact that the Soviets will be even more devastated does not lessen the misery that Americans would experience.

Option 3 Set up a quarantine to prevent any offensive weapons from reaching Cuba.

This option offers a firm response to the Soviets without actually firing any weapons. A quarantine would be less provoking and less likely to escalate into a nuclear exchange than the first two options.

The quarantine increases the American advantage by putting the confrontation on the sea, where America's strongest forces would be battling the weakest branch of the Soviet military. Then the conflict might be limited to just one or two ships and not be viewed as an invasion of a sovereign nation. Within two days, U.S. Navy warships

President John F. Kennedy (1917-1963) and
Secretary of Defense Robert McNamara (right) meet
at the White House.

can put a 2,100-mile ring around Cuba to intercept any
Soviet ship. Navy planes can reinforce the blockade by
searching for ships and cargo planes headed for Cuba.

One attractive feature of this option is flexibility.
At the moment, you are not certain why the Soviets tried
to get away with putting the missiles in Cuba or what
they are now thinking. This makes it difficult to predict
how they would respond to any of your actions. The
quarantine keeps new Soviet weapons out of Cuba while it
buys you time to work out some kind of peaceful solution
with the Soviets. At the same time, a quarantine leaves
open the possibility of further military action, if necessary.

The main disadvantage is that, unlike *Option 1* and
Option 2, the quarantine does not do anything about the
missiles already in Cuba: it will not solve the problem and
only delay the solution. Your military advisers and some

influential senators in your own political party do not believe the quarantine is a strong enough response.

On the other hand, the quarantine may be too strong. While it falls short of an actual attack, Soviet commanders may not accept the humiliation of an enemy boarding their ships. In order to enforce the quarantine, American ships must be prepared to sink any ship that refuses to be boarded. The sinking of any ship, whether American or Soviet, could mushroom into World War III.

Option 4 Negotiate a settlement.

Since the inferior forces of the Soviets are in a desperate position, negotiating a settlement should not be too difficult. The Soviets should be eager for a way out that will allow them to salvage some pride. The American missiles in Turkey could provide a convenient way out. You don't need those missiles. In fact, unknown to the American public, your administration considers them obsolete and has already decided to dismantle them. Offering to remove the missiles in Turkey in exchange for the removal of those in Cuba would cost you nothing.

Another possibility could be an American pledge not to invade Cuba in exchange for withdrawal of the missiles. A peaceful settlement eliminates a possible escalation of hostilities into a nuclear exchange. Many Americans would regard such a swap as a shameful sign of weakness. They might ask, "Do the Soviets just have to threaten us and we offer them a deal to stop?" An article in *Time* magazine expresses the view that the U.S. bases in Turkey are not the same as the Soviet bases in Cuba because the U.S. is not a threat to world peace and the Soviets are.

At the same time, the Soviets have given you no indication that they would accept such a swap. They have sunk a billion dollars into this Cuban missile project. With that much invested, are they likely to scrap everything so easily? What if the Soviets don't want to deal?

Option 5 **Allow the missiles to stay.**

Those in favor of this option question whether this issue is worth the risk of a nuclear war. As one adviser asks, "What's the difference between being killed by a missile from the Soviet Union or from Cuba? We're dead both ways." The Soviet threat is the fact that they have weapons, not where the weapons are located.

General Taylor speaks for many when he counters that if you fail to stand up to the Soviets when they are caught red-handed trying to sneak weapons into Cuba, you are giving them license to keep pushing their luck.

YOU ARE THE PRESIDENT.
WHAT IS YOUR DECISION?

Option 1   **Invade Cuba.**

Option 2   **Bomb the missile sites.**

Option 3   **Set up a quarantine to prevent offensive weapons from reaching Cuba.**

Option 4   **Negotiate a settlement.**

Option 5   **Allow the missiles to stay.**

Deciding how to deal with the Soviets over their missiles in Cuba was one of the biggest challenges John F. Kennedy faced as president.

President John Kennedy chose *Option 3*.

Kennedy believed he had to make a firm stand against the Soviets and their deception. At the same time, he resisted the almost unanimous advice of military advisers to bomb or invade. "It isn't the first step that concerns me," he said, "but both sides escalating to the fourth and fifth step, and we don't go to the sixth step because there is no one around to do so." Kennedy was not worried so much about what the Soviet leaders would do as he was about actions and errors beyond the control of the leaders. He wanted to show strength while at the same time give Khrushchev, the Soviet leader, plenty of time to think before taking any rash action.

At 7:00 P.M. on October 22, Kennedy informed the nation of the crisis and his response. He warned that the U.S. would regard any missile launching as a Soviet attack and would trigger a full-scale counterattack. He publicly rejected the idea of withdrawing nuclear weapons from Turkey in exchange for withdrawal of missiles from Cuba. He ordered his naval commanders to stop all Soviet ships, first by an order to halt and then with a shot across the ship's bow. The U.S. Navy was to sink any ship that failed to comply. Also, American planes would intercept all Cuba-bound cargo aircraft and force them to land in the United States for inspection. Any aircraft that refused to cooperate would be shot down.

Carrying out President Kennedy's quarantine order,
the U.S. Navy inspects a Soviet ship (in background).

RESULT

The blockade began on October 24, 1962, at 10:00 A.M.
Within 30 minutes of the start, two Soviet tankers
approached the line, stopped, and then turned around
and headed back toward their home ports. Several Soviet
ships continued to steam toward Cuba in defiance of
Kennedy's policy. On Thursday, October 25, the U.S.
Navy intercepted a Soviet tanker. They allowed the ship,
carrying a cargo of oil, to pass without inspection. On the
third day, Friday, October 26, two American destroyers
stopped and boarded a Soviet freighter. American inspec-
tors searched the ship and allowed it to continue on its way.
Following this search, the rest of the Cuba-bound cargo
ships turned away and did not challenge the quarantine.

The Soviets seemed to be complying with the quarantine. But aerial photographs showed that the Soviets were still at work on the Cuban missile sites, and they had made no moves to dismantle anything.

On Saturday, October 27, the situation was tense. That morning, the Soviets shot down an American U-2 surveillance plane. U.S. plans called for an air strike if any of its surveillance planes were shot down. Disagreeing with most of his advisers, Kennedy overruled the plan.

That night, Kennedy sent a message to Khrushchev giving the Soviets one last chance at a peaceful solution. He demanded that the Soviets remove their missiles immediately. If they did so, Kennedy would agree to a public pledge not to invade Cuba, which the U.S. had decided not to do anyway. Kennedy also privately informed Khrushchev that the U.S. had already planned to remove the missiles from Turkey. However, Kennedy warned the Soviets that if they made this information public, the deal was off. If the Soviets did not agree within 24 hours to these terms, the United States would take military action to remove the Soviet missiles.

Many of Kennedy's advisers who knew the details of the offer doubted the Soviets would take the deal. Robert McNamara said he "was not sure I'd ever see another Saturday night."

Nikita Khrushchev, however, accepted the terms in a public radio broadcast at 9:00 A.M. on October 28, 1962. The Soviets began dismantling the missiles. The crisis, which U.S. Secretary of State Dean Rusk called "the most dangerous the world has ever seen," ended without bloodshed.

A few of Kennedy's advisers believed that the quarantine and negotiation were a mistake. On hearing of the settlement, General Curtis LeMay said, "We lost. We ought to just go in there today and knock 'em off."

But that was by far a minority opinion. Even General Taylor, who had never backed down from favoring some kind of attack on Cuba, said of Kennedy's quarantine, "I'm glad he did it because it proved to be enough." Kennedy's handling of the crisis also earned widespread approval among both America's allies and the neutral nations.

Later information revealed to an even greater degree the wisdom of Kennedy's choice. Soviet General Dimitri Volkogonov has said that there were at least 20 nuclear warheads in Cuba at the time of the crisis. Further, Volkogonov put the Soviet troop strength in Cuba at 42,000—more than double the American estimate. This meant that an invasion would have proven even more costly than the American military leaders had anticipated.

Fears of Soviet reaction to being humiliated by the United States turned out to be well founded. Even the relatively mild use of force in the quarantine stung the Soviets so badly that they reacted by engaging the Americans in a costly arms race, creating enough nuclear weapons to destroy the earth several times over. Greater use of military force by the United States could well have sparked an even more aggressive reaction on the part of the Soviets.

Kennedy's fears of an accident or misunderstanding blowing the crisis into a catastrophe also appear to have been well founded. Soviet leaders apparently did not authorize the downing of the American U-2, yet that incident almost caused Americans to go to war. One Soviet general claimed that individual Soviet commanders in Cuba were authorized to fire their nuclear missiles. In the confusion of an invasion or an air attack, one lapse of judgment could have caused these weapons to be fired, triggering a full-scale nuclear war.

Also, at the height of the crisis, another American U-2 flying near the Arctic Circle lost its bearings and began heading toward Moscow. Had the tension between the U.S. and the Soviet Union been any higher at that time, the Soviets could easily have considered this lost plane an attack or at least the preparation for an attack. Again, a misunderstanding could have caused unspeakable destruction.

The quarantine succeeded because it bought time. As the crisis wore on, that time allowed Kennedy to learn more about the Soviets and to predict their response. Those few extra days, as well as a small concession on Kennedy's part, also gave Khrushchev just enough breathing room to make a rational decision in response to Kennedy's ultimatum.

7

SOUTHEAST ASIA
June 1965

The headache in Southeast Asia that you inherited from previous presidents is turning into a migraine. Despite your efforts to bolster the government of South Vietnam, it is in danger of falling to the Communists.

Communism, which is directly opposed to the capitalism of the United States, is fostered by your deadliest foes—the Soviet Union and China. Since World War II, Communist regimes have taken over Eastern Europe, China, Cuba, North Korea, and North Vietnam.

As leader of the world's democracies, the United States is committed to protecting free countries from the threat of Communist domination. Agreement is widespread among American observers that South Vietnam is a key country in the effort to stop the spread of communism.

Many cite the "domino theory" to explain the importance of South Vietnam.

According to the domino theory, South Vietnam is located at a strategic point that stands between the Communist nations of Northeast Asia and the non-Communist nations of Southeast Asia. If the Communists capture Vietnam, they will have a clear path to Thailand, Malaysia, the Philippine Islands—all the way to Australia. If Vietnam falls, the other countries will topple, one after the other, like dominoes.

Under present policy, you are offering military and economic support while the South Vietnamese do most of the fighting. The more than 20,000 American troops stationed in South Vietnam are there strictly to advise and to defend vital positions, such as air bases. But this spring, the war has been going badly. The South Vietnamese army suffered a clear defeat in a series of battles ending on May 31 and again in early June. Communist forces have grown so bold that they attacked an American base in Saigon, the capital, on Christmas Eve.

BACKGROUND

Your response to this situation is made difficult by the long and complicated history of hostilities in Vietnam. Prior to World War II, this area, known since the nineteenth century as Indochina, had been under the control of the French. Following the war, the people of French Indochina, like many people in the countries in Africa and Asia, demanded their independence from European domination. Of the numerous groups fighting for independence in Vietnam, the strongest group was the Vietminh led by Ho Chi Minh.

As World War II was ending, the major powers got together, hoping they could prevent another war by deciding how the world should look. In general, the United States supported independence movements in European colonies. But when the French, backed by the British, insisted on retaining control of their colony, the U.S. agreed because they were uneasy about Ho Chi Minh's Communist leanings.

After initial sporadic fighting between the French and the Vietminh, a deal was reached in which Vietnam would become a free state in the French Union. On March 31, 1946, Ho Chi Minh left Vietnam for Paris to discuss the final details. As soon as he left, the French colonialists in the south split the country in two, declaring the South would remain under their control. Ho Chi Minh in France was unable to prevent this. Frustrated, he returned home to Hanoi, where the French were already trying to reassert their control. It was only a matter of time before fighting broke out again.

Between 1949 and 1953, the United States gave more than two billion dollars to the French in their battle to hold onto Indochina. Ho Chi Minh's independence movement wore down France's will to fight, and the French withdrew from Indochina in 1954.

At that time, a ceasefire was negotiated—largely between the French and Chinese, who generally ignored the Vietnamese—that divided French Indochina into North and South Vietnam. Ho Chi Minh and his supporters governed North Vietnam; a non-Communist regime ruled South Vietnam. This ceasefire was only intended to be temporary. Elections were to be held throughout Vietnam in 1956, but the South Vietnamese government was unwilling to take part in the election and cancelled them. The South Vietnamese then appealed to the U.S. for assistance. Unwilling to allow a possible Communist victory, the U.S. started supporting South Vietnam. Those in the North backed efforts by South Vietnamese Communists (with the division of Vietnam, the Vietminh in the south became known as the Vietcong) to gain control over the South Vietnamese government and to unite North and South Vietnam into one country.

The United States had made a treaty with the South Vietnamese government in 1954 to help the country in case of attack. American leaders viewed the Communist threat against South Vietnam as just such an attack. President Eisenhower sent several hundred military advisers to aid South Vietnam in its defense, as well as economic aid to help stabilize the country.

Communist pressure against South Vietnam increased. In 1960, the Communist party of North Vietnam publicly called for the liberation of South Vietnam. The Vietcong stepped up their efforts to gain control of rural areas and began a campaign of terror against local officials. President Kennedy responded by committing more and more American support troops to South Vietnam. By mid-1962, they numbered 12,000.

The situation grew more desperate. The South Vietnamese government fell into disarray when officers of the army overthrew and killed President Ngo Dinh Diem.

The Vietcong controlled an estimated two-thirds of the South Vietnamese rural areas. They were supported by military supplies flowing down the Ho Chi Minh Trail from North Vietnam.

At every step of the way, the United States answered the ever-increasing danger to South Vietnam with greater force. This has happened so gradually that you find yourself at war with no formal declaration. After a report of a North Vietnamese attack on an American ship in neutral waters in August 1964, Congress gave you the power to "take all necessary measures to repel any armed attack against the forces of the United States and to prevent further aggression." After Communist forces killed American soldiers in two attacks in February 1965, the United States began regular bombing of North Vietnam.

Everything has happened so gradually that you now find yourself mixed up in a dangerous fight without Congress having declared war.

THE DECISION IS YOURS.

South Vietnam is losing the war, and American troops now in that country are at risk. What will you do?

Option 1 Pull out of South Vietnam.

Undersecretary of State George Ball argues that you should get out before matters get worse. You are one step away from committing yourself to a large-scale land war in Southeast Asia. Many factors work against you in fighting such a war: great distance from home, unfavorable jungle terrain, a weak ally, and an unfamiliar culture.

Southeast Asia, 1965

CHINA

BURMA

LAOS

• Dien Bien Phu

Hanoi • • Haiphong

GULF OF TONKIN

Rangoon •

Vientiane •

NORTH VIETNAM

THAILAND

Khesahn • • Hue

Tchepone

• Da Nang

Bangkok •

CAMBODIA

Nha Trang

Phnom Penh •

SOUTH VIETNAM

Saigon •

SOUTH CHINA SEA

MALAYSIA

INDONESIA

• Kuala Lumpur

SINGAPORE
Singapore

Even if your military performs well, Ball sees "no assurance that the United States can gain its political objectives" by fighting a land war in Vietnam. Your political objectives are to help South Vietnam develop a strong, stable, democratic government. Unfortunately, the government you are supporting in South Vietnam is neither strong nor stable, nor does it enjoy the unquestioned support of the people. Unanswered questions about the involvement of the U.S. in the assassination of President Diem make some Vietnamese believe that the present South Vietnamese government is just another tool of the foreign colonial masters—in this case, the United States. How will propping up the present government with foreign soldiers bring about the trust of the people? What right do Americans have to stick their noses in someone else's business? Why should you send Americans to die in Asian jungles in another country's war?

You have no moral obligation to defend South Vietnam with a large military effort. The Southeast Asia Treaty Organization (SEATO) pact that the U.S. signed in 1954 required you to aid and defend South Vietnam in case of an open invasion. But you cannot exactly describe the present conflict as an open invasion. The Communists believe the conflict is just another step in their long battle for the independence of their country. Many of the South Vietnamese, the side you are supposedly fighting for, are Communists. As of 1964, an estimated 170,000 South Vietnamese Vietcong are fighting against the South Vietnamese government.

Suppose you do decide to continue backing South Vietnam in this war. How do you win such a war? An army normally gains advantage by taking enemy territory. That would not be possible here. The Vietcong fight a guerrilla war; they attack and then melt into the jungle to resurface somewhere else. You can move in troops to clear an area of enemy soldiers, but the enemy just goes into hiding. As soon as you leave, they return. If taking territory is not a legitimate goal, what exactly are the goals of your military effort? How do you "win"?

Ironically, John Kennedy stated the problem clearly in his days as a senator, before he became involved in prosecuting the war: "To pour money, material, and men into the jungles of Indochina without at least a remote prospect of victory would be dangerous, futile, and self-destructive."

Option 2 Ask Congress to declare war on North Vietnam and use whatever military means necessary to win the war.

Pulling out of Vietnam would be a shameful act, a violation of the pledge made by the United States to stand with the government of South Vietnam. Senator William Fulbright of Arkansas has said that an "unconditional withdrawal would betray our obligations to people we have promised to defend." Senator Thomas Dodd says that the United States cannot back out of its commitments because the "defense of the free world depends on American power and determination."

Secretary of State Dean Rusk carries that argument even further. He says that the consequences of not facing up to aggression are "enormous and dangerous." If the United States breaks its commitments in Vietnam, then "our word is no good." Rusk maintains that the

As chairman of the Senate Foreign Relations Committee from 1959 to 1974, William Fulbright (here shaking hands with President Lyndon Johnson) cautiously approached U.S. intervention abroad.

Communist world would draw conclusions from that cowardly action "that would lead to our ruin and almost certainly to catastrophic war."

Furthermore, the American people would probably not forgive you. A great many people are already upset because the U.S. has not responded to Communist aggression in Eastern Europe. These same people are disappointed because their government settled for less than total victory in Korea. Recent Gallup polls show fewer than one out of five Americans believes the United States should withdraw from Vietnam.

The peace negotiations conducted since the French left have proven useless. The best thing to do, then, is to show the North Vietnamese what war really is. The United States should declare war on the Communists and aim for complete victory. By having Congress officially declare war, you would not give your enemies the opportunity to label this "the president's war." You would have the Congress solidly behind you.

Secretary of Defense Robert McNamara has said that "we will do whatever is necessary to achieve our objective." So why tiptoe around? The objective is to keep South Vietnam from being taken over by Communists. The Vietcong Communists would not be a serious threat if North Vietnam did not support and supply them. Your objectives would be best served by bringing North Vietnam to its knees. The United States has built up such an arsenal of military firepower that it could "bomb North Vietnam back to the Stone Age," as Senator Barry Goldwater has said. Some generals believe that you should not rule out nuclear weapons in this war against North Vietnam.

Option 3 **Reinforce American troops but continue using them only to defend vital installations.**

The last thing you want to do is follow Goldwater's advice. He was your opponent in the last election, and his aggressive talk about bombs scared the voters during the campaign. You took a more peaceful approach, saying that "we don't want our American boys to do the fighting for Asian boys." Voters overwhelmingly preferred your policy and elected you in a landslide.

Entering the international arena with too big a chip on your shoulder is dangerous. If American troops so much as cross the border into North Vietnam, much less start lobbing nuclear bombs at them, they had better be prepared to take on the Chinese and possibly even the Soviets, who are allies of North Vietnam. China boasts the largest army in the world. The Soviet Union, of course, owns enough nuclear weapons of its own to destroy the United States.

Even the simple step of asking Congress to declare war on North Vietnam contains potential pitfalls. A firm

Barry Goldwater, the unsuccessful Republican presidential candidate in 1964, advocated strong military measures against the Vietnamese Communists.

declaration of war might spook China, North Vietnam's neighbor, into entering the fighting. At the other end of the spectrum, suppose Congress did not go along with your request for a declaration of war? Then your hands would be tied. You would have to halt all operations and withdraw troops immediately. Vietnam would be lost.

The best solution is to continue to let the South Vietnamese army do the bulk of the fighting while American troops seal off and protect vital areas such as air bases. This strategy has three main advantages: First, it is the option that best upholds the integrity of the South Vietnamese government. Were U.S. troops to take over the fighting, this would become America's war. The United States would be taking over most decisions, running the war and the country. Even if this brought success, the South Vietnamese people could then view their government as America's puppet. That status would further hinder the South Vietnamese government's effort to win the trust of the people.

Second, this option gives the American military the most workable goal. The question was asked earlier: How could the United States demonstrate a clear victory in the war if your strategy did not allow your troops to take territory from an enemy? This option eliminates the need to gain a victory. All that the United States needs to do is avoid losing. The Vietcong might continue to defeat the South Vietnamese in some battles but would be unable to capture South Vietnam because they would not be able to take those decisive areas controlled by American forces. Eventually, the futility of their effort would discourage them and cause them to seek a peaceful settlement.

Finally, this option allows the United States to live up to its commitments with the smallest loss of American life. The disadvantage to this option is that it hasn't worked in the past and it puts the U.S. troops at a disadvantage by only allowing them to defend themselves.

Option 4 **Increase American troop strength and actively take part in the fighting against the Vietcong.**

The recent defeats of the South Vietnamese armies show why you cannot just continue your present policy of defending certain vital installations. In two bloody defeats, American troops were in the vicinity of the fighting. Had they been called in to support the South Vietnamese, they could have turned the tide of battle. What is the sense in having troops ready and available and then not allowing them to win battles for you?

Furthermore, your present strategy puts American soldiers in great danger. Troops defending certain areas are sitting ducks waiting for the Vietcong to launch their sneak attacks. A more active defense would allow American patrols to clear the area of hostile forces and disrupt enemy movements.

The grim military situation in Vietnam is a result of the Vietcong and the North Vietnamese increasing their efforts at military and government infiltration. You must meet this with increased force of your own, as two American presidents before you have done whenever the enemy has stepped up its attacks.

Maxwell Taylor, the American ambassador to South Vietnam and an ex-general, believes you must take a more

General William Westmoreland (at microphones) believed that strongly increasing the number of U.S. soldiers in Vietnam would prevent the country from falling to the Communists.

active role in the war. He calls the present strategy "a rather inglorious static defense mission, unappealing to them (United States forces), and unimpressive in the eyes of the Vietnamese."

General William Westmoreland, commander of American military forces in Vietnam, agrees that the current strategy is not working. He describes the South Vietnamese army as "near collapse." How can the American army offer support if there is no effective army to support? At least for the present, American troops will have to take over the fighting before the country is completely overrun.

Westmoreland recommends "beefing up" the United States forces to 180,000 men and "taking the fight to the Vietcong." That should be enough to stabilize the situation and prevent a takeover. Once that is done, you will need additional troops to defeat the enemy. Westmoreland estimates that you could accomplish this objective by the end of 1967.

YOU ARE THE PRESIDENT. WHAT IS YOUR DECISION?

Option 1   **Pull out of South Vietnam.**

Option 2   **Ask Congress to declare war on North Vietnam and use whatever military means necessary to win the war.**

Option 3   **Reinforce American troops but continue using them only to defend vital installations.**

Option 4   **Increase American troop strength and actively take part in the fighting against the Vietcong.**

President Lyndon Johnson chose *Option 4*.

Presidential aide Bill Moyers noted that "the president was less a hawk than any man in the government" and would do almost anything to avoid involvement in a large-scale war. He agonized about sending Americans to fight overseas. Conversely, Secretary Rusk's points about the consequences of "running out" on an ally swayed Johnson. "We will stay until aggression has stopped, because in Asia and around the world are countries whose independence rests, in large measure, on confidence in America's word and in America's protection," the president declared.

Johnson accepted Westmoreland's recommendation of greatly increasing U.S. strength and taking a more offensive role in the war in Vietnam. On July 28, 1965, Johnson gave Westmoreland the authority to commit the U.S. Army's ground forces to fighting wherever needed in South Vietnam. A month later, he approved the total deployment of 180,000 soldiers.

THE RESULT

The United States found itself stepping from the slippery footing of its early Vietnamese policies into a bottomless bog. Month by month, the fighting continued to escalate. Johnson sent more and more troops to stem the Communist tide. By the end of Westmoreland's estimated timetable for victory, more than one-half million American soldiers were patrolling South Vietnam and flying bombing missions over North Vietnam. Despite optimistic reports from the field, a peaceful end to the

President Johnson visits the soldiers in Vietnam, with General Westmoreland (in cap) at his side.

conflict was no closer than it had been when Johnson made his decision to take an active part in the war.

In the U.S., public support for the war eroded, and protests and draft card burning became common. The Vietnam War sparked more domestic unrest than the country had experienced since the Civil War. Facing challenges from war critics in his own party and discouraged by his inability to grasp either peace or victory, Johnson declined to run for a second full term in 1968.

After Johnson left office, the war dragged on for four more years before the Americans finally pulled out, declaring South Vietnam strong enough to stand on its own. That belief was wrong. On April 30, 1975, the North Vietnamese overran Saigon, the capital of South Vietnam, and took control of the entire country.

Worn out by the Vietnam War and American public demonstrations against it, President Johnson (1908-1973) left the White House in January 1969, with the end of the fighting nowhere in sight.

The Vietnam War sparked protest from many Americans who wanted U.S. troops to return home.

HINDSIGHT

Historians consider Johnson's Vietnam policy a failure. His administration failed to understand the nature of the war: that the matter of winning the hearts and minds of the Vietnamese was more important than killing the enemy. Johnson and his advisers underestimated the astounding ability of the North Vietnamese to absorb punishment, particularly the bombing of their cities. Long past the point when most nations would have been expected to give up and seek peace, the North Vietnamese kept fighting.

By not asking Congress to declare war, Johnson saddled himself with the full responsibility for the fighting. Johnson failed to muster the support of the American people—support that he needed to carry out his policies.

Finally, the domino theory proved to be largely a myth. After the fall of Vietnam, Communist forces did not sweep through all of Southeast Asia. The fighting in Vietnam did spill over into Laos and Cambodia, and Cambodia became engulfed in factional fighting for many years. The worldwide Communist movement ended with the defection of Eastern Europe and the breakup of the Soviet Union in the late 1980s.

But Johnson was not alone in failing to foresee the consequences of his decision. At the time he made the choice, the American people supported him. As late as March 1966, 50 percent approved of his handling of the war, and only 33 percent disapproved. Carroll Kilpatrick, the White House correspondent for the *Washington Post* during the Johnson years, said that Johnson "was doing what almost any president at the time might have done."

The difficulty of the crisis that Johnson faced is easier to understand if one considers that, two decades later, the people of the United States were still divided as to what he should have done. A 1990 poll reported 54 percent thought the U.S. should not have sent troops. About 36 percent thought the U.S. should have gone all out to win the war.

Nevertheless, as president, Johnson took the blame. The loss of more than 58,000 lives in a failed effort to defend South Vietnam overshadowed his astounding effectiveness in guiding social and civil rights legislation through Congress.

8

A THIRD-RATE BURGLARY
June 1972

Your campaign for a second term as president had just kicked into high gear when a bizarre news incident aroused the public's curiosity. In the early morning hours of June 17, a security guard discovered a burglary in progress at the national headquarters of your rival political party in the Watergate complex. The guard called local police, who arrested five men. The burglars appeared to be installing telephone-bugging devices.

Because of the possibility that the burglars broke federal communications laws, the Federal Bureau of Investigation (FBI) entered the case. Later that day, the FBI determined that one of the burglars was James

McCord, who happens to be chief of security for your Committee to Re-elect the President. A search of a suspect's hotel room then turned up a check signed by E. Howard Hunt. Hunt, curiously, had worked for White House aide Charles Colson in late March. Questioned about these developments, your press secretary dismissed this incident as "a third-rate burglary," not worthy of comment.

You had no knowledge of the planning and execution of this break-in. But as the facts of the matter become clear, you discover some things about it that make you uncomfortable.

BACKGROUND

The men who carried out the Watergate break-in are part of a special investigative unit under the direction of your White House aides. This unit is commonly known as the "Plumbers" because their original function was to stop government officials from "leaking" information to the press.

These leaks of classified information had frustrated you and hampered your ability to govern. The public disclosure of a 7,000-page document known as the *Pentagon Papers* finally pushed you past your limit. In 1971, the *New York Times* published excerpts from these classified papers that revealed the stories behind a number of secret governmental decisions pertaining to the Vietnam War. Soon afterwards, you learned that Daniel Ellsberg, a former National Security Council employee who opposed the war, had leaked the *Pentagon Papers*.

Investigators of the Watergate burglary linked E. Howard Hunt to the crime.

You tried to get a court order preventing the newspapers from printing these government secrets, but the Supreme Court turned down your request.

You believed that the constant leaks of classified information, the strong protests of the antiwar movement, and the lenience of the courts combined to threaten law and order in the United States. In response, you created the Plumbers to wage a secret campaign to protect national security. The Plumbers have since engaged in a variety of secret activities, such as investigations and wiretaps of the president's enemies. This includes a break-in at the office of Ellsberg's psychiatrist in a search for information that would discredit Ellsberg, as well as the forging of cables that would link President Kennedy with the assassination of South Vietnamese President Diem.

Further, this special investigative unit has, at your request, gotten involved in this presidential campaign. Although you have been running well ahead of all challengers, your campaign takes nothing for granted. You expect the opposition to engage in the sort of "dirty tricks" you have seen in past elections, and you are determined to beat them at that game. You told your staff to come up with "imaginative dirty tricks" to "annoy, harass, and embarrass the opposition—as [you have] been in the past." They responded with a number of ploys, such as investigating the families and acquaintances of rival candidates and forging embarrassing letters in their names.

However, some of your closest aides believe you need more secret information in order to keep your campaign opponents on the defensive. H. R. (Bob) Haldeman and Charles Colson put pressure on the Committee to Re-elect the President for more intelligence operations. One of the results of this pressure was the plan to bug the party headquarters at Watergate, where White House Plumbers became involved.

If some of these secret bugging operations were discovered, you were prepared to cite a tense national security situation and the Omnibus Crime Control Act of 1968 as the bases of your conduct. This law included a provision asserting the president's power to use electronic surveillance to prevent the overthrow of the government. But as luck would have it, just two days after the Watergate break-in, the Supreme Court ruled that this power is subject to the Fourth Amendment, which

Presidential adviser Charles Colson

requires court approval before authorities can search or seize private property. None of the operations carried out by your Plumbers had this prior court approval.

That leaves you wide open to investigations into the Watergate affair that could be extremely embarrassing to you and could bring out into the open this pattern of shady, unethical, and even illegal activity of the Plumbers that you condoned. Your excuse that you were engaging in dirty tricks only because the other side was doing it would look flimsy without evidence to support your argument.

Furthermore, some of your closest friends are mixed up in this Watergate affair. You have learned that G. Gordon Liddy masterminded the break-in. Liddy reported directly to John Mitchell, the chairman of the Committee to Re-elect the President. Mitchell is a long-time friend who also served as your attorney general. Mitchell probably approved the break-in plans. Both Haldeman and Colson had some involvement in these intelligence operations. They may or may not have been directly involved in criminal activity, but either way, public knowledge of their roles could cost them their jobs. John Ehrlichman, another trusted aide, was closely involved in the Ellsberg burglary.

Coming in the thick of an election campaign, the timing could not be worse. Polls show that you are so far ahead of your opposition that the whole Watergate break-in was unnecessary. If the White House connections to the seamy nature of the Plumbers become known, what will this do to your election chances?

G. Gordon Liddy, *chief planner of the Watergate*
burglary

THE DECISION IS YOURS.

As the investigation into the Watergate burglary intensifies, what actions will you take?

Option 1 **Cooperate fully with the investigation and accept the consequences.**

As embarrassing as this whole incident may be, you could only make it worse by trying to cover it up or by pretending it doesn't exist. At the moment, you are guilty of nothing more than errors in judgment. If you withhold information or block an investigation, however, you could possibly be guilty of obstructing justice, which is against the law.

The best policy for an effective government is honesty. Far better to cut your losses, come clean, answer all questions honestly, admit mistakes, and apologize to the American public if necessary. The people may even gain greater respect for you because of your integrity, and you will maintain your self-respect. Even if the American public does not appreciate your honesty, full cooperation will get this whole Watergate affair behind you. The public may forget it in a matter of weeks, and you would be able to get on with your work without having Watergate consume your time and energy.

If anyone presses you about any shady dealings of the Plumbers that might be exposed, you can simply explain that, while mistakes in judgment may have occurred, you believed this type of operation was necessary for the security of the nation in a difficult time.

This option has two problems. What if the American people do not forgive and forget? As a rough-and-tumble politician, you have made a great many enemies over the years. If you meekly give in and cooperate with this investigation, your enemies may take that as a sign of weakness and seize the opening to destroy you.

The second problem with this option is that while you may come out of it in fine shape, your aides may not be so lucky. If John Mitchell actually did authorize the Watergate break-in, then he is guilty of a crime. Are you willing to cooperate in putting a close friend and the former attorney general—the symbol of law and order in your administration—in jail? Are you willing to take the chance that investigators will link Haldeman, Ehrlichman, Colson, and others to specific crimes that resulted from the Plumbers' operation?

John Mitchell with his ex-law partner Richard Nixon

Option 2 **Cooperate fully with the investigation and grant pardons to those in your administration who are indicted or convicted.**

Option 1 would be disloyal to those who did nothing more than faithfully carry out your wishes to the best of their ability. You can't just walk away from your friends while they pay the price.

The solution to your problem lies in Article II of the Constitution, which gives the president the "power to grant reprieves and pardons for offenses against the United States, except in cases of impeachment." Why not use that power to pardon those involved in the incident? After all, the people who served you are not criminals. Perhaps they got carried away and went a little overboard at times. But whatever they did, they did for the right reasons—because they believed that their actions were helping their country.

Watergate is no big deal. You have been involved in politics long enough to realize that dirty tricks have been a part of national politics for a long time, and you suspect that you have been on the receiving end of far more than you have dished out. Some of your supporters suspect that voter manipulation in razor-close voting in Texas and Illinois cheated you out of victory in the 1960 presidential campaign against John Kennedy. Politics is a rough game, and the break-in is just part of the way the game is played. Chances are the other party is spying on your campaign organization, too.

The American people recognize this fact of life. A fresh poll shows that an overwhelming majority of Americans, 70 percent to 30 percent, feel that tapping another party's headquarters is acceptable political spying. Why then would anyone object if you grant a pardon for any technical violations of law that may have occurred, citing the tremendous good these public servants have done for their country?

Pardoning political friends, however, has seldom been sound strategy in the United States, and you should use pardons cautiously. The president is supposed to uphold the laws of the country and see that these laws apply to everyone. Arguing that you are applying the law fairly when your friends get off the hook for actions that would put anyone else in jail is a difficult task. The public could react with outrage.

Option 3 Cover up evidence of White House involvement in Watergate.

Admitting blame and cooperating fully in an investigation that embarrasses your administration may sound noble, but such a plan could also be political suicide. Your best chance to be an effective president is to limit the investigation so that the dirty tricks and the sordid conduct of the Plumbers are not made public. Although you may justify what you have done by citing national security needs, this would be a public relations disaster. You could end up looking sleazy, mean spirited, and even incompetent.

Haldeman and Ehrlichman, your closest advisers, are cautioning you against taking that chance. As the most powerful leader in the world, you certainly have the means to keep the White House connection to Watergate hidden. For example, you can ask the Central

Intelligence Agency to keep the FBI from digging further into the case. Warn the FBI that they have come upon a secret CIA operation and that their investigation is blowing the CIA's cover. That should be a plausible story because several of the Watergate burglars are anti-Communist Cubans with CIA connections.

The only way that investigators can learn the whole story behind the Watergate break-in and the Plumbers unit is if someone on the inside tells them. You have only seven people to worry about—the five burglars and their immediate superiors, G. Gordon Liddy and E. Howard Hunt, whose guilt is obvious. The FBI already has enough evidence to convict them, so the federal agency no longer needs to continue its probe. As long as none of the seven talk, the investigation will go no further. All these men are strongly devoted to your presidency.

If your White House aides happen to fall under suspicion, they do not have to answer any questions that you don't want them to answer. When investigators get too close to sensitive areas with their prying, you can invoke "executive privilege." (Executive privilege is the president's right to withhold information if he or she believes secrecy to be in the public interest.) While investigators could challenge this fuzzy legal principle in court, the federal courts have historically shied away from confrontations with the president.

Finally, respect for the office you hold will work to your benefit. Even if the FBI and the American people begin to question some of your actions, they will both give your story the benefit of the doubt. As Ehrlichman

John Ehrlichman (above) and H.R. Haldeman, the president's top advisers

says, "You gotta go on the assumption that the American people want to believe in their president."

Despite all the advantages of your office, this is a risky option. Covering up a crime and hindering a criminal investigation are illegal. If you choose to go this route and by some rare stroke of bad luck are ever found out, then you are in big trouble. Congress could impeach you and convict you of violating your oath of office. This would force you to resign the presidency. No president in the history of the country has ever suffered such humiliation.

Option 4 **Stall the investigation until after the election and then cooperate.**

With your considerable power, you may be able to squelch the investigation. However, if just one thing goes wrong, the whole plan may unravel. The Watergate burglars may resent going to jail for following orders while those who gave them those orders get away scot-free. One of your aides may start feeling the heat from investigators, then panic and start talking to save himself. The courts may reject your claims of executive privilege and force you to supply information, too.

None of these possibilities is likely to happen right away. But the longer the cover-up lasts, the greater the odds that something will slip out of the bag. The most realistic strategy might be to delay the investigation a few months until after the November election.

Your main opponent in the upcoming election is a man whom you consider dangerous. Most of your associates regard this candidate as a bungling radical who would weaken the security of the country, cave in to the anti-establishment "hippies," sacrifice Vietnam to the Communists, and weaken American defenses. They believe he does not support the values held by the "silent majority" of Americans. His views appear to be so far from the mainstream that he has alienated even many traditional supporters of his party. You view his election to the presidency as a frightening prospect. John Mitchell agrees, saying that your election "is the most important thing to this country."

Voters are a fickle lot. If the facts about the Plumbers are put before them, your opponent may find a way to use that to his advantage. This revelation may even turn the election in his favor.

Once you are in office, you can afford the negative press and the loss of popularity that will come with any Watergate investigation. You will have the power to carry out your programs. Once the initial reaction to Watergate wears off, the American people will appreciate what you have done for them as president.

YOU ARE THE PRESIDENT. WHAT IS YOUR DECISION?

Option 1   **Cooperate fully with the investigation and accept the consequences.**

Option 2   **Cooperate fully with the investigation and grant pardons to those in your administration who are indicted or convicted.**

Option 3   **Cover up evidence of White House involvement in Watergate.**

Option 4   **Stall the investigation until after the election and then cooperate.**

President Richard Nixon chose *Option 3*.

Nixon did not want to suffer the embarrassment of seeing the undercover actions of his administration exposed. He later explained, "I didn't believe we were covering any criminal activity. I saw Watergate as politics, pure and simple. We were going to play it tough." Playing it tough meant what he called "stonewalling"— keeping the truth from the investigators.

As for the idea of letting his aides take their punishment for what Nixon admitted were "stupid" actions, Nixon claimed he was guided by loyalty. "I was never a good butcher," he said. He rejected the idea of pardons as bad politics.

On June 23, 1972, Nixon and Haldeman agreed to steer the Watergate investigation away from any links between the burglars, the Committee to Re-elect the President, and the White House. They decided to use the CIA to warn the FBI away from investigating further. They assigned White House assistant John Dean to the task of planning and carrying out a program that would block the Watergate investigation.

At various times, Nixon wrestled with the idea of what he called the "hangout" route—coming clean and telling all he knew. But both at the beginning and after the election, he always backed off into what he called a "modified, limited hangout"—half-truths and incomplete information.

President Richard Nixon (1913-1994), who had practiced hard-nosed politics since the 1940s, chose not to reveal the extent of White House involvement in the Watergate burglary and cover-up.

RESULT

Under Dean's direction, the cover-up succeeded for nine months. Nixon captured more than 60 percent of the popular vote in defeating George McGovern in the November 1972 election. As of April 1973, Nixon's approval rating among the American people held at nearly 60 percent.

But even during this time, signs of trouble appeared. E. Howard Hunt demanded large sums of money in exchange for keeping silent. That involved the president

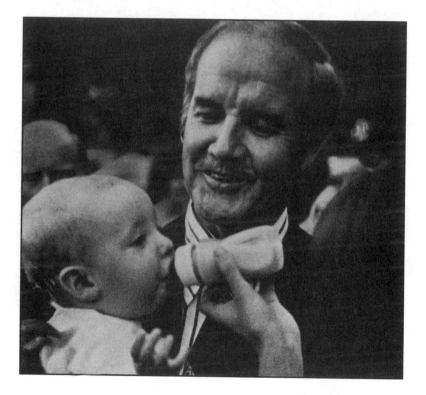

Senator George McGovern of South Dakota campaigned unsuccessfully for the presidency in 1972.

White House aide John Dean

and his staff in raising illegal "hush money." The *Washington Post* pursued the Watergate story relentlessly. Despite Dean's efforts, investigators learned that John Mitchell committed a crime by approving the Watergate burglary plans.

The cover-up started to unravel in March 1973 when James McCord, hoping to avoid a jail term, began cooperating with authorities. As investigators drew nearer the truth, White House aides began to worry that they would end up being a scapegoat for the president. Loyalty to Richard Nixon took a back seat to personal survival. The biggest defection was from John Dean, who in April 1973 decided to tell what he knew—which was just about everything. Senate and criminal investigators closed in. By May, Haldeman, Ehrlichman, Dean, Mitchell, and several others were indicted in federal court on criminal charges.

Nixon managed to avoid the net that closed around his aides. As Ehrlichman had predicted, the American people held to their belief in their president. In August 1973, despite growing suspicions of Nixon's involvement

North Carolina Democrat Sam Ervin (center) led the Senate's investigation of the Watergate affair.

in a cover-up, a majority of Americans continued to give him the benefit of the doubt.

Nixon's downfall came when word leaked out that he had tape-recorded all conversations in his Oval Office. Investigators asked for tapes of certain conversations as evidence about what had been discussed in the White House about Watergate. At first, Nixon refused, citing executive privilege. Eventually, though, he lost the battle on two fronts: the public wondered what he was hiding by not supplying the tapes, and, finally, the Supreme Court rejected his claim of executive privilege and ordered him to surrender the tapes.

The June 23, 1972, tape was the "smoking gun" that proved Nixon had involved himself in obstructing justice almost from the beginning of Watergate. With his impeachment and conviction by Congress assured, Nixon resigned the presidency at noon, August 9, 1974.

As new President Gerald Ford and his wife, Betty (left), say goodbye, former First Lady Pat Nixon and Richard Nixon prepare to board the helicopter that will take them from the White House.

Nixon very nearly pulled off his strategy of deception. Had he not secretly tape-recorded all his conversations, had that fact not been inadvertently revealed by an aide, and had the Supreme Court ruled in his favor on the tapes, he probably would have survived what one prosecutor called "the greatest constitutional crisis since the Civil War."

Newspaper columnist James Kilpatrick, a Nixon supporter, believed that Nixon could have easily solved his problem by telling the truth. "Had he told the truth from the outset," Kilpatrick wrote, "Watergate would have been a nine-day wonder, Nixon would have been reelected, and no more would have been heard of the affair." As it was, Watergate destroyed his presidency.

Although he had difficulty admitting the extent of his wrongdoing, Nixon realized the folly of his decision to cover up Watergate. He once stated, "Overzealous people often do wrong in campaigns. What really hurts is if you try to cover it up."

"I let the American people down," Nixon concluded. "I have to carry that burden with me for the rest of my life."

SOURCE NOTES

Quoted passages are noted by page and order of citation:

pp. 10, 12, 17 (1st, 4th), 18 (2nd), 19, 24: Irving Greenberg, *Theodore Roosevelt and Labor: 1908-1919* (New York: Garland, 1988.)

pp. 13, 16, 17 (2nd, 3rd), 18 (1st), 22 (2nd): William Henry Harbaugh, *Power and Responsibility: The Life and Times of Theodore Roosevelt* (New York: Farrar, Straus & Cudahy, 1961.)

pp. 22 (1st, 3rd, 4th): Theodore Roosevelt. *Autobiography* (New York: Scribner, 1958.)

pp. 27, 28, 34, 40 (1st, 2nd, 4th, 5th), 43: Gene Smith, *When the Cheering Stopped: The Last Years of Woodrow Wilson* (New York: Time-Life, 1966.)

p. 32: August Heckscher, *Woodrow Wilson: A Biography* (New York: Scribner 1991.)

p. 40 (3rd): Arthur Walworth, *Woodrow Wilson: World Prophet.* (New York: Longman's, Gren & Co., 1958.)

pp. 46, 48 (1st), 52, 55, 58: James MacGregor Burns, *Roosevelt: The Soldier of Freedom* (Harcourt, 1970.)

p. 48 (2nd): Henry Steele Commager and Milton Cantor, *Documents of American History, Vol. I* (Englewood Cliffs, NJ: Prentice Hall, 1988.)

p. 49: Kenneth S. Davis, *FDR: Into the Storm, 1937-40* (New York: Random House, 1993.)

pp. 70, 72 (1st, 2nd), 76 (1st): David McCullough, *Truman* (New York: Simon & Schuster, 1992.)

pp. 72 (3rd), 76 (2nd): Robert H. Ferrell, *Truman: A Centenary Remembrance* (New York: Viking Press, 1984.)

pp. 81 (1st), 82 (1st), 88, 90: Piers Brendon, *Ike: His Life and Times* (New York: Harper & Row, 1986.)

pp. 81 (2nd), 82 (2nd), 85, 87: Robert Burk, *The Eisenhower Administration & Black Civil Rights* (Knoxville: University of Tennessee Press, 1984.)

pp. 101, 105, 108 (3rd): James G. Blight, Joseph S. Nye, and David Welch, "The Cuban Missile Crisis Revisited" (*Foreign Affairs*, Fall 1987.)

p. 108 (1st, 2nd): J. Anthony Lukas, "Class Reunion" (*The New York Times*, August 30, 1987.)

p. 115: *The Vietnam War: Opposing Viewpoints* (San Diego: Greenhaven, 1990.)

pp. 117, 124: Larry Berman, *Planning Tragedy* (New York: W.W. Norton, 1992.)

pp. 118, 120 (1st), 126: Henry F. Graff, *The Tuesday Cabinet* (Englewood Cliffs, NJ: Prentice Hall, 1970.)

p. 120 (2nd): Merle Miller, *Lyndon: An Oral Biography* (New York: Putnam, 1980.)

pp. 132, 134, 143, 152 (1st, 2nd): Stanley I. Kutler, *The Wars of Watergate* (New York: Knopf, 1990.)

pp. 146, 152 (3rd): David Frost, *"I Gave Them a Sword"* (New York: Morrow, 1978.)

BIBLIOGRAPHY

Brendon, Piers. *Ike: His Life and Times.* New York: Harper & Row, 1986.

Burk, Robert. *The Eisenhower Administration & Black Civil Rights.* Knoxville: University of Tennessee Press, 1984.

Burns, James MacGregor. *Roosevelt: The Soldier of Freedom.* Harcourt, 1970.

Committee on the Judiciary of the House of Representatives. *Impeachment of Richard Nixon.* New York: New York Times Co., 1975.

Ferrell, Robert H. *Truman: A Centenary Remembrance.* New York: Viking Press, 1984.

Greenberg, Irving. *Theodore Roosevelt and Labor: 1900-1918.* New York: Garland, 1988.

Harbaugh, William Henry. *Power and Responsibility: The Life and Times of Theodore Roosevelt.* New York: Farrar, Straus & Cudahy, 1961.

Heckscher, August. *Woodrow Wilson: A Biography.* New York: Scribner, 1991.

Karnow, Stanley. *Vietnam: A History.* New York: Viking Press, 1983.

Kutler, Stanley I. *The Wars of Watergate.* New York: Knopf, 1990.

Lukas, J. Anthony. "Class Reunion," *The New York Times*, August 30, 1987.

McCullough, David. *Truman.* New York: Simon & Schuster, 1992.

Miller, Merle. *Lyndon: An Oral Biography.* New York: Putnam, 1980.

Reedy, George. *Lyndon Johnson: A Memoir.* New York: Andrews & McMeel, 1982.

Smith, Gene. *When the Cheering Stopped: The Last Years of Woodrow Wilson.* New York: Time-Life, 1966.

Thompson, Robert Smith. *A Time for War.* New York: Prentice-Hall, 1991.

INDEX

American Federation of Labor, 18

Arkansas, school integration in, 79-81, 82, 84, 85

Arkansas National Guard, 90

Article II (U.S. Constitution), 140

atomic bomb: decision to use during WW II, 66-70, 72; development of, 61-62; opposition to use of, 70; power of, 62, 63, 67, 70, 101; used on Hiroshima, Nagasaki, 72-73, 74, 75

Bacr, George, 13, 15, 16-17

Ball, George, 115, 117

Bay of Pigs invasion, 96

Bock's Car, 73

bombing cities as weapon in war, 46, 64-65, 66, 67, 68-69, 70, 72-76

Borah, William, 27

Brown v. The Board of Education of Topeka, 77, 79, 85, 88, 89

Castro, Fidel, 96

Central High School (Little Rock, Arkansas), 79-81, 91

Central Intelligence Agency (CIA), 93, 98-99, 141-142, 146

Churchill, Winston, 46, 47, 48, 58, 69

Civil War, 83

Clemenceau, Georges, 42

Cleveland, Grover, 16, 17

coal industry, 11-12

coal mine owners, 11, 14, 15, 20, 23; attitudes of, toward strike, 10, 13, 14, 16, 17, 19

coal miners, 9, 10-17; strike of, 9, 10, 11, 13, 16, 17, 20, 22, 23; working conditions of, 11-12, 17, 23

Colson, Charles, 132, 135, 136, 139

Committee to Re-elect the President, 132, 135, 136, 146

communism, 93, 94, 96, 111

Constitution, U.S., 10, 19, 24, 28, 77, 84, 89, 140

Covenant of the League of Nations, options in winning approval of: leaving vote to Senate, 37-38; taking case to people, 31-34; withdrawing proposal temporarily, 37; working out compromise with Senate, 34, 36

Cuba: and Bay of Pigs invasion, 96; quarantine of, by U.S., 106-108; relationship of, with U.S., 93, 96; Soviet missile sites in, 93-94, 95-96, 97, 105-106, 108, 109

Cuban missile crisis, options for ending of: allowing missiles to stay, 104; bombing missile sites, 99-101; invading Cuba, 97-99; negotiating settlement, 103-104; quarantining Cuba, 101-103, 107, 109-110

Davies, Ronald, 79
Dean, John, 146, 148, 149
Dodd, Thomas, 118
"domino theory," 112, 130

Eastland, James, 78
Ehrlichman, John, 136, 139, 141, 142-143, 149
Eisenhower, Dwight, 70, 88; attitude of, toward states' rights, 89, 92; belief of, in compromise, 90, 92; and use of federal troops in Little Rock, 89-91; and Vietnam conflict, 114
Ellsberg, Daniel, 132, 134, 136
employees, rights of, 11, 14-15, 19, 20
Enola Gay, 72, 73
"entangling alliances," 48
Ervin, Sam, 150
executive privilege, 142, 144, 150

Fat Man, 69, 73
Faubus, Orval, 79-80, 81, 86, 89
Federal Bureau of Investigation (FBI), 131-132, 142, 146
federal government: power of, 24; and states' rights, 82, 87
federal troops, 16, 22-23, 24; use of, to enforce school integration, 82-83, 86, 89, 90, 91
Ford, Betty, 151
Ford, Gerald, 151
Fourteenth Amendment, 77
Fourth Amendment, 135-136
Fulbright, William, 118, 119

Germany, 25; during WW II, 45, 46, 50, 52, 54, 55, 56, 58, 59, 62
Goldwater, Barry, 120, 121

Great Britain: and Lend-Lease Act, 59, 60; need of, for war material, 46-48, 50, 53, 58, 59; struggle of, against German forces, 45-46, 50, 56, 58, 59; request for aid during WWII, options in responding to: doing everything short of war, 49-52; entering war on Great Britain's side, 54-55; turing down request for aid, 55-56; working around loopholes in Neutrality Act, 53-54

Haldeman, H.R. (Bob), 135, 136, 139, 141, 143, 146, 149
Hiroshima, 72-73, 76, 101
Hitler, Adolf, 44, 45, 61, 92
Ho Chi Minh, 113
Ho Chi Minh Trail, 115
House, Edward Mandell, 34, 35, 36
Hungary, 86
Hunt, E. Howard, 132, 133, 142, 148

Indochina, French, 112, 113
integration, school, 78-81, 84, 85, 91
Iwo Jima, battle of, 64

Jackson, Andrew, 86-87
Japan: atomic bomb used on, 72-73; 75; attack of, on Pearl Harbor, 59, 60, 100; effect of war on, 62, 65; surrender of, 75; and war with U.S., 62-63, 64, 65-66
Japanese surrender, options in bringing about: bombing and blockading Japan, 64-66; demonstrating power of atomic bomb, 66-68;

dropping atomic bombs on Japanese industrial cities, 68-70; invading Japan, 63-64
Jefferson, Thomas, 48
Johnson, Hiram, 53-54
Johnson, Lyndon, 119, 127, 128; and escalation of Vietnam War, 126-127, 129-130

Kennedy, John, 102, 140; decision of, to quarantine Cuba, 105, 106-110; negotiations of, with Khrushchev, 106, 108, 110; and Vietnam conflict, 114, 118, 134
Khrushchev, Nikita, 99, 106, 108, 110
Kilpatrick, Carroll, 130
Kilpatrick, James, 152
King, Martin Luther, Jr., 92

La Follette, Robert, Jr., 54
Lauterbach, Edward, 18, 19
League of Nations: Covenant of the, 26, 28-29, 30, 31, 36, 37, 41-42; end of, 43; opposition to, 26, 27-28, 29, 30, 34; origins of, 25, 26; support for, 26, 29, 37; U.S. role in, 34, 36, 37, 43, 48
LeMay, Curtis, 109
Lend-Lease Act, 59, 60
"lend-lease" plan, 53, 54, 58, 59, 60
Liddy, G. Gordon, 136, 137, 142
Lindbergh, Charles, 55, 59
Little Boy, 68, 73
Little Rock school integration crisis, 79-81, 90, 91; leaving state to handle, 82-84; sending federal troops in, 86-

87; working out compromise with local officials, 84-86
Lloyd George, David, 42
Lodge, Henry Cabot: and coal strike, 10, 18; and League of Nations, 26, 29-30, 36, 42

McCone, John, 93
McCord, James, 131-132, 149
McGovern, George, 148
McNamara, Robert, 101, 102, 108, 120
Manhattan Project, 61-62, 70
Mann, Woodrow Wilson, 81, 85, 87
Marshall, George, 56
Mitchell, John (chairman of Committee to Re-elect the President), 136, 139, 145, 149
Mitchell, John (President of United Mine Workers union), 13, 17, 18
Monroe Doctrine, 27
Moore, James, 17
Moyers, Bill, 126

Nagasaki, 73-74, 75, 76, 101
Nazis, 50, 51, 54, 56, 58, 62
Neutrality Act, 48, 51, 53, 58
Ngo Dinh Diem, 114, 117, 134
Nixon, Pat, 151
Nixon, Richard: resignation of, 150-151; and Watergate, 139, 146-150; and Watergate tapes, 150, 152
North Vietnam, 113-114, 119, 120, 121, 126
Northern Securities Corporation, 19
nuclear weapons, 95-97, 98, 101, 106, 109, 110

Okinawa, battle of, 64

Omnibus Crime Control Act, 135

Orlando, Vittorio Emanuele, 42

pardons, power of president to grant, 140

Pearl Harbor, attack on, 59, 60, 65, 100

Pennsylvania coal strike: causes of, 13; effect of, on nation, 9-10, 14, 16; end of, 23; negotiations in, 13, 17, 19-20, 23

Pennsylvania coal strike, options in ending of: pressuring both sides to negotiate settlement, 19-20; sending federal troops to break strike, 14-16; sending federal troops to seize mines, 16-18; staying out of dispute, 19

Pentagon Papers, 132

"Plumbers," 132, 134, 135, 136, 138, 139, 141, 142, 145

Pullman, railroad operators strike of, 16, 17

Republican party (in South), 83-84, 85, 88, 92

Roosevelt, Franklin, 24, 57, 59, 60; death of, 61; "Four Freedoms" speech of, 58; and "lend-lease" plan, 53, 58, 60; and Manhattan Project, 61-62

Roosevelt, Theodore, 21; role of, in ending miners' strike, 22, 23, 24; and threat to use federal troops, 22, 23

Root, Elihu, 22

Rusk, Dean, 108, 118-119, 126

Russell, Richard, 92

Schofield, J. M., 22

segregation, 77-78, 80, 83, 85, 86, 89

"separate but equal doctrine," 77

South Vietnam, 113-114; Communist threat to, 111-112, 114, 120; fall of, 127; U.S. aid to, 112, 114, 117; U.S. military forces in, 114, 115, 126

Southeast Asia Treaty Organization (SEATO), 117

Soviet Union, 86; and building of Cuban missile sites, 93-94, 97, 105; and nuclear arms race, 96-97, 109-110; reaction of, to quarantine of Cuba, 106, 107, 108; relationship of, with Cuba, 93-94; on WWII, 59

Special Investigative Unit, 132, 134

"Square Deal," 24

states' rights, 82-83, 86-87

Stevenson, Adlai, 89

Stimson, Henry, 49-50

Stone, William, 13

submarines, German, 46, 52, 53

Supreme Court, 77, 78, 84, 85, 86, 88, 89, 134, 135, 150, 152

Taft, William H., 36

tapes, Watergate, 150, 152

Taylor, Maxwell, 98, 104, 109, 123-124

Truman, Harry, 6, 7; attitude of, toward use of atomic bomb, 72, 76

Turkey, U.S. missiles in, 97, 103, 106, 108

unions, 13, 14, 15, 17, 18, 23

United Mine Workers, 13, 14, 17, 18, 23

United Nations, 43
U-2 surveillance plans, 108, 110

Vietcong, 114, 115, 117, 118, 120, 122, 123
Vietminh, 113, 114
Vietnam, background of conflict in, 112-115
Vietnam conflict, options in dealing with: declaring war on North Vietnam, 118-120, 121; pulling out of South Vietnam, 115, 117-118; using U.S. troops to fight Vietcong, 123-125, 126-127, 128; using U.S. troops to protect vital installations, 120-123
Volkogonov, Dimitri, 109

Warren, Earl, 89
Watergate burglary, 131-132, 135, 136, 142; cover-up of, 146-149; investigation of, 149-150; planning of, 136, 137; tapes relating to, 150, 152; options in dealing with: cooperating with investigation and accepting consequences, 138-139; cooperating with investigation and pardoning those convicted of crime, 140-141; covering up evidence of White House involvement, 141-144; stalling investigation, 144-145
Watson, James, 34
Westmoreland, William, 124-125, 126, 127
Wheeler, Burton, 59
Wilkie, Wendell, 49

Wilson, Woodrow: 33, 35, 39, 42, 48, 54; background of, 39; efforts of, to win support for League, 40-41, 43; health of, 40, 41; as public speaker, 41
World War I, 25, 27, 42, 43, 48, 52, 55, 72
World War II, 43, 45, 46; atomic bomb used during, 72, 73, 74, 75, 101; casualties during, 64, 65; cities bombed during, 64-65, 72-73, 74, 75, 76; Germany in, 45, 46, 50, 52, 54, 55, 56, 58, 59, 62; Great Britain in, 45, 46, 48, 50, 52, 53, 56; Japan in, 59, 61-66; U.S. involvement in, 48-49, 51-52, 54-55, 59, 60, 61-63, 98

ABOUT THE AUTHOR

NATHAN AASENG is an award-winning author of over 100 fiction and nonfiction books for young readers. He writes on subjects ranging from science to business, government to law. Aaseng's books for The Oliver Press include *America's Third-Party Presidential Candidates, Genetics: Unlocking the Secrets of Life, Great Justices of the Supreme Court, Treacherous Traitors, You Are the Corporate Executive, You Are the General, You Are the General II: 1800-1899, You Are the Juror, You Are the President, You Are the President II: 1800-1899, You Are the Senator,* and *You Are the Supreme Court Justice.* He lives in Eau Claire, Wisconsin, with his wife and children.

Photo Credits

Photographs courtesy of the Harry S. Truman Library: pp. 6, 74; Library of Congress, pp. 12, 15, 18, 21, 29, 33, 39, 44, 47, 50, 60, 71, 78, 121, 147; National Archives, pp. 27, 52, 66, 68, 69, 73, 75, 133, 135, 137, 139, 143 (both), 148, 149, 150, 151; Seely G. Mudd Manuscript Library, Princeton University Libraries, pp. 35, 42; Franklin D. Roosevelt Library, p. 57; Associated Press, pp. 81, 91; Dwight D. Eisenhower Library, pp. 88, 90; John Fitzgerald Kennedy Library, pp. 94, 99, 102, 105, 107; Lyndon Baines Johnson Library, pp. 119, 124, 127, 128; UPI/Bettmann, p. 129.